Portraits of A Virtuous Woman

The Woman God Called YOU to Be

Cynthia E.J. Carter

"Igniting Moral Perfections Through Literature."

No part of this work may be reproduced or transmitted in any form or by any means electronic or mechanical, including photocopying and recording, or by any information storage or retrieval system, except as may be expressly permitted by copyright acts or in the writing from the authorized representative of the author.

Request for permission should be addressed to:

Cynthia E. J. Carter

P. O. Box 23200

Houston, Texas 77228-3200

or by E-mail: cynthiaejcarter@att.net

Copyright © 2001, 2005, 20008 and 2010

ISBN13:9781539324591

by Cynthia E. J. Carter

ISBN10:1539324591

Second Edition: Library of Congress Card Number: 2005904070

Published by: Virtuous Books

P. O. Box 23200, Houston, Texas 77228-3200

www.cynthiacarterministries.net

www.wutsministries.org

Scripture quotations are taken from the King James Version of the Holy Bible unless otherwise noted.

TABLE OF CONTENTS

DEDICATIONS

This book is dedicated to: First, the King – eternal, immortal, invisible, the only wise God who deserves all praise, glory, and honor. He is the one who afforded us the riches of His word for life everlasting.

Every woman of God that helps make up the body of Christ and is searching to be perfected in Him.

The man that will teach these freedoms and truths for the healing of God's daughters and the strengthening of the weak.

All mankind that they may see the grace of God and His redemptive power.

My very lovely daughter, Ayasha D. Greene; Granddaughters – Ayanna Greene and Datriuana King; Goddaughters – Calista Addo and Pascaline Okadigwe; and my nieces – Tiffany Broussard, Erica Cossey, Symphony Whitfield, and Terrica Watkins, that you all may grow appreciating the unique call of God upon your lives as virtuous women.

Lastly, the loving memories of my best friend, role model, my heart – My Mother, Johnnie Mae Whitfield (1940 - 1994). The woman who inspired me to continue no matter what. Never have I seen such courage in life, display of love for others, and devotion toward family and God, than that of my mother. I respected every step of my mother's life, especially her walk with God, and growth in the Gospel of Jesus Christ.

ACKNOWLEDGEMENTS

Pastors Robyn & Marilyn Gool – Victory Christian Center

Words limit my heart and soul felt expressions of your fervent deposits into my life and ministry. Thank you both for – walking in integrity; being obedient; being accessible to mentor, train and build leaders; and your unselfish sacrifices and dedication to the Gospel of Jesus Christ. My soul "explodes" in resounding praise for God's gift to mankind through your ministry. I pray to walk in such a manner always.

Pastor Richard Heard – Christian Tabernacle

Pastor Heard, with all my heart, I thank you for the integrity of your ministry that pours from you and that cultivates the people that God places within your pathway. Truly, I am grateful that God allowed my life to encounter your leadership and be blessed by it. I pray that as I am one of many who have benefited from your ministry, you will be proud of this representation of your compassion for a lost and dying people to be saved, delivered, and healed by the power of the Holy Spirit.

Mama Page

Thank you for being there with me through the most difficult stage of my life. I am so thankful to have a second mother to share my life. You are one in whom I have a great deal of trust and admiration, just as if you gave birth to me. I love you.

Cheryl Swinson

A virtuous woman whom labored with me in prayer almost daily over three years, to give birth to this book, as well as, other concerns of God's Kingdom work. I praise God for you being a part of my life.

Sylvia Swain

Thank you for your involvement in the birth of Word Under The Stars Ministries, Inc. "WUTS". Your assistance will always be appreciated.

Each of the following women shared their talents with me during the birthing process of this book and inspired some of the revelations written therein: Mother Mary Parker, Pastor Sandra Mosley, Evangelist Deloris Mayshack, Evangelist Barbara J. Still, Norma Williams, Pamela Horton, Cynthia Churchman, Celia Mattax, Teresa Cossey and Julia James.

To A Host of Friends and Family...

Thank you for whatever part you played in helping the completion of this book. I praise God for you.

PORTRAITS OF A VIRTUOUS WOMAN

My Ten Confession Testimony: The Revelation to Birth This Book

I went to a Women's prison in Florida to preach a revival. While walking and talking to the prisoners on the grounds, some of the most hardened women prisoners watched me and observed my countenance, my physical make-up, and my feminine characteristics. They came to the conclusion that I could not possibly identify with their struggles, nor offer them hope for restoration and confidence in God's ability to forgive them, love them and even use them. One of the women asked, "Have you ever been in prison?" My answer was "No. But, I have seven brothers and five of those seven have been incarcerated. And, I added, I did some of the things that it would have taken to get here, but by the grace of God, I did not get caught."

That night, because I shared with those women freely, God truly was able to work great miracles there in the service. Over 300 women came to the services during that weekend, and we were allowed to lay hands on them and anoint them with oil. The Holy Spirit descended upon them and God began a great work in their hearts during the revival services as they received the ministering of the Holy Spirit for their own lives. I am convinced that the anointing to destroy yokes of bondage, strongholds, chains, and to heal broken hearts lie with the true witness of our lives. If I had just said, "No", and had not taken the opportunity to expound on God's grace towards me, they would not have received the Word of God through me with gladness and God would not have been able to minister life as He did those nights of the revival. That is why I testify.

The purpose of this testimony is to paint a very vivid reality of one being able to overcome strongholds, failures, compromises, and struggles and still be called a virtuous woman by God through His grace and tender mercies. As I wrote this testimony, I was tempted to omit some of the most embarrassing and humiliating events of my life from the text. However, the desire of Sir Holy Spirit is to reach far beyond the daughters of God and gain the souls of those women who can identify with my testimony. To help them believe that there is hope in their becoming all that God has predestined them to be while they were yet in their mother's womb. Therefore, like the woman called "Moses", Harriet Tubman, who revisited slavery after freedom to free others, I revisit my past to help lead the way out of the scarlet stained bondage of women into the ultimate call of their virtuous image.

> Rev. 12:11 says, "And they overcame him by the blood of the Lamb, and the word of their testimony; and they loved not their lives unto the death. "

I'm not perfect, but I am totally delivered, healed, and set free! Therefore, I share freely from my spirit, as I have freely received from Sir Holy Spirit, these words of life. I pray that the women of God will sow seeds of this revelatory book into the lives of saved and unsaved women. I trust the Holy Spirit to minister life and life more abundantly through the revelation of this book and use it as a tool to bring freedom to those who desire to be led to God's best for their lives.

I felt myself to be everything but a virtuous woman.

One morning I woke up and had no idea of who Evangelist, Cynthia Carter was. The feeling really wasn't new but this time, all of my hope was gone. A host of my shortcomings, failures, and trials flashed before me flooding my soul with depression, despair, and disgust. Even my romantic hope of becoming a vital part of the Body of Christ and making a significant contribution to the advancement of the Kingdom of God was disappointedly gone. I had sinned and that sin caused devastation in my home, ministry, and relationships.

I was guilty as charged. I did not want to sin but I did. I did not want to compromise, but I did. It was my whole life's pattern. I could do great for years at a time but over and over again, I was making some horrible, seemingly irreversible blunders in life. Everyone else knew it and had no reservations about letting me know that they knew it. I thought, "God I don't want to do this anymore! What's the point? I keep having hope, only to get hope knocked down over and over again with disappointment. This time, I don't want to do this! I don't want to be an evangelist! I will be a Christian and witness one on one as I go, but I don't want to be in ministry! I don't want to speak, teach, or anything like that! In fact, God, I don't want to live here. If I can't live exactly holy, walking in full peace, and have complete joy, I don't even want to live. I have felt embarrassed, humiliated, talked about, misused, abandoned by my brothers and sisters, and oh yea... sinners are still trapped in sin like me! I don't want to go anymore!"

I want to tell you, even as a powerful, Spirit filled, born again believer, you may experience the same attack of hopelessness and wanting to quit. Some of the most powerful prophets of the Lord experienced the desire for death, as opposed to pressing forward to the high call of God in Christ Jesus. Let's take a brief look at a few of them:

Moses said, "I am not able to bear all these people alone, because it is too heavy for me. (v15) And if thou deal thus with me, kill me, I pray thee, out of hand, if I have found favor in thy sight; and let me not see my wretchedness". Numbers 11:14-15

Look at what the great prophet Elijah did, But he himself went a day's journey into the wilderness, and came and sat down under a juniper tree: and he requested for himself that he might die; and said, It is enough; now, O Lord, take away my life; for I am not better than my fathers. I Kings 19:4

These were two of the greatest prophets that ever lived. Moses was used by God to implement the plagues upon Egypt in Pharaoh's rebellion to let His people go from bondage. He parted the Red Sea with only a rod in his hand and led the Children of Israel across on dry land. He talked with God personally, and saw the backside of God. And, that is not all; you can read more about him in the Book of Exodus. Yet, Moses went to God about the burden of his life's calling to lead and resolve other people's problems. He felt it was too much to handle and God gave him direction and provided him with what was needed, so that he could continue in life.

Likewise, Elijah, at one time, could laugh in the face of the enemy and call down fire from heaven to consume his enemies (I King 18-19). Without a doubt, Elijah's obedience, courage, confidence, and boldness in the work of God was surely displayed in the events of his life. However, after his great victory over the prophets of Baal, Elijah was so weak and worn out from the spiritual and physical battles he had engaged in, that fear gripped him when Jezebel threatened his life. Fear caused Elijah to run and isolate himself and wish for death. God saw him there and had compassion on him to "send" the angel with bread and water to strengthen him for the rest of his life's journey.

Thank God, He is faithful to provide a way of escape for us. So, whatever trials or tribulations we face, we can bear them (I Cor. 10:13). Just like Moses, in order to live, we must communicate all of our concerns to God and be willing to obey his instructions. When the time comes, like Elijah and we do not have the strength to fight, the Lord will supernaturally provide life sustaining nourishment through His Word and by His Spirit to strengthen and preserve us until the Day of Christ. Now, I know you might be thinking... "Moses and Elijah obeyed God. They just got tired." I had the same thoughts and turned it into an argument with God!

Next, there is myself, Prophetess, Evangelist, Teacher, Preacher, and Minister -- Cynthia Carter. Without hesitation, I echoed the same sentiment of both these great prophets:

"I am not like my forefathers; this is too hard for me!

Do I know anything? Life is too hard!"

My justification was - Moses and Elijah were both obedient servants of God and were fulfilling the call of God on their lives but they just got tired. I, on the other hand, was a saved sinner! I went on to rehearse my life's history before the Lord and summarized the top ten reasons why I could not be a virtuous woman as follows:

1. "Lord, I Grew Up in The Cafe Life."

I grew up in a place called "The Independent Grove". On weekends and holidays, most of the family's entertainment came from the family and locally owned cafes. There was Molly's Place (owned by my stepfather's sister), Dave's Place (owned by an aunt), and three local cafes the Blue Room, Cunningham's Café, and the Cowboys Inn. Each Cafe had an enchantment of its own and shared turns in the patronage from the surrounding communities. No one was restricted from the atmosphere. There was drinking, dancing, baseball, cards, 8-ball pool, dominoes, rodeos, sexuality, drunkenness, tempers flaring, fighting, and yes, even shootings. Still, this appeared to be the life and everybody, through the eyes of a child, appeared to live it and love it. This atmosphere opened the gates and coached me into a promiscuous lifestyle. However, in the midst of all of this, Jesus began to knock on the doors of my heart.

2. "There Are Others Who Can Do This Better."

I remember when the spirit of inferiority and discouragement attacked. My mother made us go to church every Sunday. During one Easter season, I had to learn the 23rd number of Psalms for my Easter speech. These were the very first scriptures I learned. I had to recite the speech along with another person. We both learned it, but the other young lady was so bold and courageous in reciting the psalms. I stood frozen in my place, never to forget the embarrassment.

One family at church had several girls in it. Including their mother, who was the church musician, they made up most of the choir. Boldly, their spiritual gifts shined through for everyone to see. As for me, I was the only girl out of seven brothers and I felt left out.

Once, I remember my whole family (mom, dad and my seven brothers) sitting down that night together to watch Jesus of Nazareth. Alone, I cried throughout the entire movie. From that point on, dreams took place almost every night. An angelic atmosphere appeared to surround me at all times, pointing out things to me, watching over, and protecting me. I didn't know what it was. Nor, did I discuss it with anyone. Naively, I enjoyed it. However, this did not stop or deter what I thought was the destructive course of my life. I had no real goals or ambitions (even in school). I just kind of existed.

Consequently, a spirit of inferiority and depression came upon me by the age of twelve. Yet, there remained a false sense of pride in me regarding my personal appearance. I thought I was attractive and all the men and boys confirmed it with their flirts and propositions. I was very mature in every other way but very naive in sexual matters.

3. "Lord, I'm Not a Virgin."

The day came when we moved from the country to the city. I knew my life would never be the same. We had a brand new home and I finally had a room of my own. At last, a girl my own age lived just across the street. Unfortunately, in comparison to me, she was just a little girl playing with dolls.

I was the second child of eight and the only girl. I had a lot of motherly duties because my mother was oftentimes a "live-in maid". Everything I said and did was in the image of a mature woman since all the girls I chose to hang around back in the country ("The Independent Grove") were always significantly older than me. When I was growing up, I can only remember playing with dolls on very rare occasions.

Mama could never bring herself to talk to me about becoming a maturing young woman or sexuality. All I knew was, "everybody was kissing somebody." At the age of thirteen, I met an eighteen-year-old boy whom I went to a house party with down the street. I thought kissing was just fine and I was finally being accepted as a woman. On the way home that night, he date raped me. I could not bring myself to tell my mother, but I told my friend, who was like a cousin to me. Unfortunately, all of the intimate things that I learned came from older peers, who were between 16-20 years old and already sexually active. Thank God I did not get pregnant! Tragically, it did get worse, I quit school.

4. "I quit school in the eighth grade. I'm uneducated!"

"I can't be like the girl across the street", I said to my mother who could not understand why. I felt like a misfit, caught between age and maturity. Therefore, school was not where I wanted to be. Peers my own age only added to my frustration. We appeared to be worlds apart in our concepts of life.

Mama wanted to pray and wish all of her concerns away. She did not know how to communicate with me. After the rape, I did not return to school. Every morning I left the house pretending to go to school. In reality, I was skipping school to go to work. I put my age up and found a job. All this time my mother believed it was a part-time job that I was working only after school. Needless to say, by the time my mother found out, I had missed so many days from school that it was too late.

I had dropped out of school. And, I upheld the family tradition of a cafe lifestyle. At this point, only the entertainment had changed. Its influence was strong enough for me to leave home at age thirteen (soon to be fourteen).

5. "I left home at thirteen and God, you know the people

I was around and all that I did..."

The added cafe attractions were exotic dancers and these dancers became my friends. I was now fourteen, lying saying I was eighteen. I decided that even though I wasn't doing the same things my friends were doing, it was OK for me to move out of my mother's house and move into an apartment with them. I was working at a truck stop restaurant as a waitress. Eventually, I stopped going to church and became a waitress in a bar where my friends worked.

6. "Lord, I have danced in a bar..."

It was the wrong time for me to be offered to do the wrong thing. "Try it just once", my friends encouraged. "No one will know", I thought. After all, I was among strangers. I tried it once, and that was once too many .

As soon as I stepped on the dance floor in my skimpy outfit, in came the cameras taking pictures for the club's advertisement. Humiliated and disgusted with myself, I ran from the stage. Later, a thirty-four-year-old man, who put me up in an apartment and bought me a car, befriended me. At that time, my parents had no idea where I was. But, that all changed when someone gave a copy of the advertisement to my parents. Consequently, my mother seized an opportunity to bring me home. Juvenile showed up at the door to take me to detention. Hallelujah!

At the time I was furious. My thoughts were, "How dare she send Juvenile after me. I am not a little girl!" Somehow, I made it through the night in the Detention Center. I was released to my mother the next day with a threat from Juvenile officials, not to leave home before eighteen again, or they would lock me up for a longer period.

My friend came to meet my mother and he asked her permission to marry me but she flat out refused. Angry, I kept asking her, "Why not?" All she would say was, "I can't let you." We both cried ourselves to sleep that night.

The next day, all I could think of was, I was not like the girl across the street, who was the same age as me. She giggled, played with dolls, and had crushes on boys her own age. She was a cheerleader in school and had a relationship with her parents. I was now sixteen, dating no one less than twice my age, driving cars with no license, smoking cigarettes, and I did not know how to have a relationship with my family, or people my own age.

Disappointed in myself, I tried to commit suicide by taking all kinds of pills. I went in the closet of my room with no one knowing I was in the house. With both hands full of pills, I took all of them. Fortunately, God's grace stepped in and I woke up the next morning. Although I remained high for about three days, I was in my right mind.

Finally, I reached out to God, and was saved completely at age seventeen. I went back to church and started teaching Sunday school. Still feeling void, I felt I had nothing going for me except my looks. I was already soiled and there was no way to become innocent again, or wash away all the crud and grime that I felt inside.

7. "Lord, Remember Divorce #1?"

At eighteen, I married my "first" husband. He was tall, dark, and handsome. "Yes... he was!" And, he was only four years older than I was. I felt so thankful that he was interested in me. I was in love, ready to settle down, and have a family. On the other hand, my husband had not begun to experience anything close to what I had overcome. We were years apart in maturity.

After the first year of marriage, somehow my husband, for whatever reason, began to use drugs excessively. The fights began both physically and mentally. Blackened eyes, cracked ribs, pulling guns, you name it -- it happened. During this time, three children were born to us. And, for ten years the cycle of abuse continued.

As a young Christian and as a mother, I really wanted my marriage to work. But, it appeared the more I prayed, the worse things got. Finally, the answer came. Job 33:15-16 reads: (v15) In a dream, in a vision of the night, when deep sleep falleth upon men, in slumberings upon the bed; (v16) Then he [the Lord] openeth the ears of men, and sealeth their instructions.

The Lord showed me in a dream with my children and me wading in some extremely troubled water. I warned my children to get out of the water because the currents were so strong that they would be pulled under and drown if they kept going. However, I kept wading into the water. Even though I could swim, I knew that if I kept going, the fierceness of the currents would pull me under. I woke up knowing without a shadow of a doubt that the dream referred to my marriage.

God sets before us life and death and then encourages us to choose life (Deut. 30:19). One of three things was going to happen: I was going to kill him; he was going to kill me physically, or spiritually; or, I was going to die returning to the world as a backslider. I chose the way of escape that God had provided. The Lord provided me this passage of scripture,

I Cor. 10:12-14: (v12) Wherefore let him that thinketh he standeth take heed lest he fall. (v13) There hath no temptation taken you but such is common to man: but God is faithful, who will not suffer you to be tempted above that ye are able; but will with the temptation also make away to escape, that ye may be able to bear it. (v14) Wherefore, my dearly beloved, flee from idolatry.

Everyone cannot leave an unsaved spouse. You must be led by the Spirit of God. His voice cannot be mistaken. God's sheep know His voice (Jo.10:14). God can and will speak to every individual's heart on a level they can understand. When a marriage situation becomes life threatening, regardless of whether he wants to stay or not, he cannot be pleased to dwell with you. Ask him to leave or you leave. You are not under bondage in such cases. The following scriptures sum this truth up:

(I Cor 7:13-15): (v13) And the woman which hath an husband that believeth not, and if he be pleased to dwell with her, let her not leave him. (v14) For the Unbelieving husband is sanctified by the wife, and the unbelieving wife is sanctified by the husband: else were your children unclean; but now are they holy. (v15) But if the unbelieving depart, let him depart. A brother or sister is not under bondage in such cases: But God hath called us to peace.

Many reasons kept me bound in that marriage for almost ten years: fear of being alone; fear of failure; wanting him saved; wanting him to raise our children; fear of my lack of education; and fear that my children's needs would not be met. The truth was none of this mattered! None of these concerns were protected, secured or completely met by me staying in that marriage. It is recorded in the Word of God over 100 times to "fear not." When I resolved within myself to trust God, He met every one of my needs.

Many things took place after this divorce, all of which I cannot tell in this testimony. Although, I will add, I did exercise my responsibility in addressing my deficiencies. This included my lack of education, employment, housing needs and most of all, my spiritual need for a closer relationship with God. And, I don't mean the kind of relationship that you only pick up God in your hour of need. God became my lifestyle. He progressively and miraculously opened doors for me that otherwise, if dependent upon my own ability, would not have been opened. The next excuse I provided God with was pointing at my second failed marriage.

8. "I married that second husband, even after you spoke to me..."

"You do not want to marry him!" I heard the Holy Spirit speak loud and clear on my wedding day (even as I was driving on the way to the church). There were many factors that should have prevented this marriage from taking place. But, the most important reason I will focus on is because the Lord spoke to me audibly the day of my wedding. My response was, "Lord, why didn't you tell me this before my wedding day?" At that point, the Holy Spirit immediately departed from me and so did my peace.

The Lord had been trying to tell me this all during courtship, but I ignored all of the warning signs. Once I arrived at the church, I found that nothing had gone as planned. The flowers and the church decorations had not been completed. The flower girl's shoes presented another problem, and the wedding was delayed not one hour but two and a half hours. To top it all off, there was no unity candle. When I looked out and saw the many guests, I could not bring myself to call off the wedding. Of course, I lived to regret that I did not listen to the Holy Spirit that day. I should have suffered the temporary embarrassment and called the wedding off. Instead, I had to face yet another horrible shame.

9. "I'm Guilty as Charged."

I could not believe that my second marriage was failing. He married me but we never became one in unity. He had every access to my life and everything I owned. Yet, he remained in obscurity and lived evasively with me in almost every one of his activities. Although he did not physically abuse me, he ignored all of my concerns. He did not use abusive language, but he refused to communicate with me. He came home every night, but he also left every morning no later than 7:00 a.m. and returned home no earlier than 12:00 midnight (ninety percent of the time). Others believed we were financially secure. The truth was I paid nearly all of the bills, if not all of them. My spirit was in ruination because my marriage was failing for a second time. So, I began to earnestly seek God for direction.

As I sought the Lord for direction, a host of dreams about my marriage invaded my sleep. On several occasions, I dreamt I was ministering heavily under the anointing of the Holy Spirit and that thousands of people were coming to be baptized and give their hearts to the Lord. But, my nakedness half showed because my husband would not cover me with the support I needed. These dreams revealed the true nature of our marriage relationship.

My husband owned his own business and after several rebukes from the Lord to leave my job, I went to work with him. On the days I did not work, I volunteered at the church. My services grew to over 40 hours a week. He also volunteered on Saturdays overseeing the inside remodeling of the church walls. Somehow, I still did not feel myself to be in unity with my husband. Every day at noon I prayed.

Once, while praying, I was caught up into a vision at the altar. I saw myself nine months pregnant and a man taking forceps, ripping apart the baby that was in my womb, and pulling it out limb by limb. In conclusion of the dream, it was revealed that the child represented our unborn ministry. For three months, I literally grieved the loss of that child at the altar, as if it had already been born and had been killed. I threw myself further into the work of the ministry.

I was thirsty and hungry for God. I wanted the anointing and the fulfillment of every vision and dream that God had ever given me. I dreamed of the anointing... I lived for the anointing to destroy everything that exalted itself against the knowledge of God. I was Conference Liaison, Youth Minister, New Members Class teacher, teaching a group of people on "How to Pray for Your Pastor" wrote and coordinated dramas, and I had keys to the church. My confidence in the ministry was vibrant, strong, energetic, and seemingly unshakable. The first leadership conference I organized was successful with approximately 500 leaders in attendance.

Volunteers were willing and cheerful workers. Men, who were not actively involved in ministry before, were actively learning how and becoming committed to prayer. With all of these great things happening in ministry, I never conceived the thought that the oncoming devastation would take place in my Christian walk.

Before I continue, I want to assure the church and the people involved that I respect their privacy and will refrain from using their names and the name of the church. This book has been written in a way to veil identities.

Furthermore, I have already asked for forgiveness of all parties involved and do apologize officially for all of my transgressions. I have also forgiven all those who have trespassed against me. Knowing that these circumstances were meant for evil but God worked them for my good and for the good of others. After these events occurred in my life, I met many women. More than I could have imagined, who had suffered the same humiliation. These women were contemplating suicide, quitting the ministry, quitting Christianity, and they were women who were tremendously suffering with the torment of guilt, shame, and condemnation. These women were trapped in the state of oppression with no one to turn to for healing, because the Church was not mature enough, or would not minister to them. In fact, most of them, like me, were asked to leave the Church. I am convinced that this part of my testimony is vital to the life of the virtuous image within these women that God still sees in them and wants to bring forth. God wants them to see themselves as He sees them and use them for his glory. With that said, I will continue to write. I was guilty as charged, humiliated, devastated, and abandoned. The charge was adultery.

A few months had gone by and my grief became obvious to my pastor. I began to share with him my marital disappointments and he began to share his personal concerns. Out of all this, an attraction grew. One thought, entertaining sin, leads to another. Who was I going to tell? Who was going to counsel me? In all honesty, this pastor had done this before and I had allowed myself to become vulnerable to his weakness, lust. It happened, "adultery".

Afterwards, one day as we talked on the phone, we discussed that this would not turn into an affair and that it would never happen again. Little did we know that my husband had recorded all of our conversations and he was not going to keep quiet about it!

I was dragged out before the people and humiliated. My husband gathered together a few ministerial leaders of the church and together they composed and sent a letter to the entire congregation. The letter called for the resignation of the pastor, as well as, exaggerated the details of what had happened. Does this remind you of the woman that was taken in the very act of adultery (John 8:1-11)? I believe I felt what she must have felt when she was dragged out before the people all in the name of the Lord, using scriptures to justify their actions. Everyone in the church knew the letters was circulating --except me.

The Saturday afternoon before finding out that the letter was circulating, I kept hearing the voice of God say, "I'M SOVEREIGN!" Over and over again, I kept hearing, "I'M SOVEREIGN!" Those words echoed so in my spirit that I could not compose myself nor stand on my feet. I had to bow down until the Lord had finished ministering His sovereignty to me. The next day, I received a copy of the letter. Moreover, in the same week, I found out that my mother was dying from cancer with only a few weeks to live. I was devastated.

I continued to go to church, even though religious stones were being thrown at me from the pulpit and the members' looks were stabbing me in the spirit. One member commented, "You still have the nerve to come here?" Well, that Sunday, I was desperate. On top of all the humiliation, embarrassment, and abandonment that I was experiencing, my mother was dying. Weeping, I went before the church to ask for prayer for my mother. No one wanted to touch me, especially not the Pastor, or his wife.

Instead of individual prayer (which was normal service), a corporate prayer was prayed for all the needs that morning. Upon taking my seat, I received a second hand word from a member that the mission sisters wanted to ask me to leave the church.

I left the church devastated that Sunday. A few weeks later, my mother died. As I took care of the funeral arrangements, I felt abandoned by the Christian community that I had loved, prayed for, gave to, and nurtured with whatever gifts I possessed.

In my hour of need, I felt abandoned by everyone who could have possibly offered me some hope. I was not making light of my sin or unwilling to bare my cross. I had said within myself, like Jeremiah, Woe is me for my hurt! my wound is grievous; but I said truly this is a grief, and I must bear it. (Jer. 10:19) I felt like Jesus must have felt when he cried out the words "being interpreted, my God, my God why hast thou forsaken me?" (Mk.15:34).

Our sins that He bore on the cross momentarily separated Him from the Father. The same people He was giving His life for crucified Him. My sin had separated me temporally from the church and my grief tried to drown out my comfort of knowing that the presence of God was with me. Graciously and lovingly though, the Holy Spirit faithfully reminded me of God's voice ministering "I'M SOVEREIGN!" to me.

These words encouraged me to know that I could trust God like Job did, He knows the way that I take: and when he has tried me, I shall come forth as gold (Job 23:10).

Finally, I compared myself to the other women in ministry and those church women, who I considered to have spiritually arrived, or at least appeared to have spiritually arrived. I then gave God the tenth reason why I could not continue in ministry.

10. "Women of God and women in ministry don't

have these kinds of problems or this kind of past."

At this point, God began to minister greatly to me about me and the call of God on my life. First, by using the prophet Elijah, He showed me how all of my excuses of wanting to quit the ministry and life amounted to evilness in His sight.

I Kings 19:9-18,

(v9) And he came thither unto a cave, and lodged there; and, behold, the word of the Lord came to him, and he said unto him, What doest thou here, Elijah? (v10) And he said, I have been very jealous for the Lord God of hosts: for the children of Israel have forsaken thy covenant, thrown down thine altars, and slain thy prophets with the sword; and I, even I only, am left; and they seek my life, to take it away. (v11) And he said, Go forth, and stand upon the mount before the Lord. And, behold, the Lord passed by, and a great and strong wind rent the mountains, and brake in pieces the rocks before the Lord; but the Lord was not in the wind: and after the wind an earthquake; but the Lord was not in the earthquake: (v12) And after the earthquake a fire; but the Lord was not in the fire: and after the fire a still small voice. (v13)And it was so, when Elijah heard it that he wrapped his face in his mantle, and went out, and stood in the entering in of the cave. And, behold, there came a voice unto him, and said, What doest thou here, Elijah? (v14) And he said, I have been very jealous for the Lord God of hosts: because the children of Israel have forsaken thy covenant, thrown down thine altars, and slain thy prophets with the sword; and I, even I only, am left; and they seek my life, to take it away. (v15)And the Lord said unto him, Go, return on thy way to the wilderness of Damascus: and when thou comest, anoint Hazael to be king over Syria: (v16) And Jehu the son of Nimshi shalt thou anoint to be king over Israel: and "Elisha the son of Shaphat of Abelmeholah shalt thou anoint to be prophet in thy room." (v17) And it shall come to pass, that him that escapeth the sword of Hazael shall Jehu slay: and him that escapeth from the sword of Jehu shall Elisha slay. (v18) Yet I have left me seven thousand in Israel, all the knees which have not bowed unto Baal, and every mouth which hath not kissed him.

Notice how none of Elijah's excuses were valid under the watchful care and control of a Holy God. Twice God asked Elijah, "What doest thou here?" Simply put, "What are you doing in this place Elijah with no hope in your heart?" God went further on to demonstrate that Satan can bring on the storms of life that can cause destruction, but not destroy us. God was not in the wind that broke the rocks into pieces. These are the rocks that seem to shake the very foundation in which our lives are built upon. God was not in the earthquake, the things that bring unstableness to our Christian living. God was not in the fire that consumes and surges away all of our confidence in the Lord of Hosts. But, we find Him and His assurance for life in His still small voice speaking to us. Twice, God asked Elijah this question, and twice, Elijah provided the same answer. In verses 10 and 14 he said, "And he said, I have been very jealous for the Lord God of hosts: because the children of Israel have forsaken thy covenant, thrown down thine altars, and slain thy prophets with the sword; and I, even I only, am left; and they seek my life, to take it away."

Then, it leaped out at me, the evilness of wanting to get out of the call of God. Look at verse 15 & 16, (v15) "And the Lord said unto him, Go, return on thy way to the wilderness of Damascus: and when thou comest, anoint Hazael to be king over Syria: (v16)

And Jehu the son of Nimshi shalt thou anoint to be king over Israel: and "Elisha the son of Shaphat of Abelmeholah shalt thou anoint to be prophet in thy room."

Elijah was prematurely seeking to get out of the call of God on his life because of what he was experiencing in his present situation. Finally, after insisting, God chose a successor, Elisha, to complete the work that Elijah did not want to finish. We see that this caused God to also change in preparation of Elisha's ministry, the whole kingship administration of His will for the people. When we look into the ministry of Elisha, what great things we see! He could hear the voice of God. He made an iron axe head swim; he caused water to flow through the land without rain; he raised a dead child; he cured leprosy; and my favorite of his works was when a dead man rose to live again from just touching his dead bones in a cave. Read about him in the Book of II Kings. These mighty acts were previously assigned to Elijah, but because he did not want to finish this race, they were passed on to Elisha.

At this point, I decided I didn't want any rocks crying out for me. I didn't want anyone else finishing the call of God for my life. I wanted Him to say, "Well done!", to me -- Cynthia. God goes on to say to Elijah, look before you quit, I want you to know, (v18) Yet I have left me seven thousand in Israel, all the knees which have not bowed unto Baal, and every mouth which hath not kissed him. God wants us to know that He does have servants who will endure to the end. Do you see what a holy and awesome God we serve and that He is able to perfect that which concerns us? Praise God!

The second thing the Lord God Almighty did was to ask me the same question, "Cynthia what doest thou hear?" I said, "I see and I hear the still small voice God." For I had a dream that I went to a women's conference. There, all of God's daughters were gathered.

As I tried to enter the door to the service, one of the leaders stretched her arm across the door to prevent my entrance. I politely moved her arm and proceeded to enter the room. Once I entered, I fell into a pit. All of the other daughters turned and gazed down at me and said, "Oh look, she fell into the swine's pit." But, I heard the voice of God say, "No! That is Joseph's pit." If you know anything about Joseph's pit, it was the pathway ordered of God to prepare and take Joseph to his destiny. Then God said, "What do you hear?" I said, I hear:

- "You made me and formed me in the womb..." Isa. 44:24
- "You called me in righteousness and you will hold my hand, keep me, and make me a light..." Isa. 42:6
- "A just man falls seven times, but riseth up again..." Prov. 24:16
- "Your hands are not too short to save... " Isa. 59:1
- "You will make me a repairer of the breach, the restorer of
- paths to dwell in..." Isa. 58:12

This continued for days, hearing the Word of God echoing in my spirit and responding to His still small voice. Finally, receiving God's challenge for life, I rejoiced in similar fashion to that of Mary, the mother of our Saviour, (v46) And Mary said, My soul doth magnify the Lord, (v47) And my spirit hath rejoiced in God my Saviour. (v48) For he hath regarded the low estate of his handmaiden: for, behold, from henceforth all generations shall call me blessed. (v49) For he that is mighty hath done to me great things; and holy is his name. (v50) And his mercy is on them that fear him from generation to generation. (v51) He that showed strength with his arm; he hath scattered the proud in the imagination of their hearts. (v52) He hath put down the mighty from their seats, and exalted them of low degree. (v53) He hath filled the hungry with good things; and the rich he hath sent empty away. Luke 1:46-53

If we are not careful to receive God's grace for our own lives and the lives of others, we may very well end up in angry bitterness, like the Prophet Jonah, who also wished for death: (v1) But it displeased Jonah exceedingly, and he was very angry. (v2) And he prayed unto the Lord, and said, I pray thee, O Lord, was not this my saying, when I was yet in my country? Therefore I fled before unto Tarshish: for I knew that thou art a gracious God, and merciful, slow to anger, and of great kindness, and repentest thee of the evil. (v3) Therefore now, O Lord, take, I beseech thee, my life from me; for it is better for me to die than to live. Jonah 4:1-3

Jonah preached to the great city of Nineveh and the whole city got saved. But, Jonah was angry about his life. God did not do things the way Jonah wanted him to. He wanted God to destroy the wicked, instead of saving them. He also hated the fact that God used him to save them. Perhaps, Jonah was envious of the grace bestowed upon the wicked. He vowed to stay angry with God and the people until his death (Jonah 4:9). Jonah's story ends with God still reasoning with him so that his soul would not be lost.

God has remembered our low estate, our shortcomings, failures, trials and tribulations, and He has had mercy on us. For those who thirst and hunger for His righteousness, you will not be sent away empty. The victory comes through fighting the good fight of faith. All of life's trials are common. We walk in them every single day!

The key is to go to God believing that He will perfect that which concerns you and present you faultless before his presence with exceedingly great joy! (Jude 24). God ministered these truths to me and called me, a virtuous woman. Something at first, I found hard to believe. Thank God, He knows where to find us and how to make us whole. Thank God that His purpose will not fail in us, as long as, we do not quit on Him. With all of this in mind, let me introduce you to "Portraits of a Virtuous Woman".

INTRODUCTION

The Woman God Called YOU to Be

Have you ever walked into the church, as a woman, searching for your role and wanting to be perfected in your Christian walk (your calling)? Knowing that you have just began your Christian walk, have you ever looked at another Christian woman who has been a long standing Christian to see if you could find the perfect model or image to portray? Have you ever looked at the Pastor's wife saying: "I wish I could be like her?" or "Is that really the way a Pastor's wife should be?" Have you ever wanted to groom your daughter like the image of the Pastor's daughter? Have you ever said, "I'm not a virgin, I have had children out of wedlock and numerous sex partners", Or "I'm not educated enough to be a virtuous woman?" Have you ever become overwhelmed with trying to find the way to become a virtuous woman? Have you ever said, "I lack charm, grace and skills?" Have you ever said, "I'm so far from the virtuous woman that I settled for a particular position in the church, feeling I didn't deserve more, or, I am unworthy of a higher calling?" Or, have you just sat down because the virtuous image seems just too hard to obtain?

Let me ask you two more questions... "Whose virtuous image in the mirror are you looking at? "And, "Are you looking in the face of another woman as if she's a mirror trying to find your own image?" STOP!! God says that no matter who you are, where you come from, what you have done, your calling is unique, single, appointed, anointed, and "yes" virtuous!

Who is the virtuous woman in this day and time? She is a woman reconciled to (1) God, (2) to man, (3) to her sister, and (4) even to herself! In these four different types of relationships, women have been estranged for many different reasons. In order to be complete in these four types of relationships, reconciliation and spiritual healing must take place.

In Portraits of a Virtuous Woman, we will focus our attention on being reconciled to God and ourselves. In doing so, we can be reconciled to man and to our sister. As the Lord ministered this word of knowledge to me and told me to put it into a book, He asked me two questions: "Who are the women of the church?" and Where did they come from?"

Then, Sir Holy Spirit took me on a Spiritual Journey. He began to bring things to my remembrance of activities in the world, in my personal life, as well as, in the lives of those I knew well. Notwithstanding, He walked me through the scriptures revealing individual lives of the plain, ordinary, common women, whose characters were brought to notable attention by the Holy Spirit and recorded in Bible. Not all of these women were of noble and humble character, but ultimately they made virtuous contributions to the Kingdom of God, significantly impacting the power of the Christian world, and helping to fulfill the divine plan of salvation to the world. These women received the highest acknowledgement that could ever be rendered. They were recorded in the Lambs Book of Life as, wise women with the ability, after repentance, to walk in the standard of virtuousness, that God set forth, for the virtuous woman, the woman of God.

As you look around the Church today, women make up about 75% of the body of Christ. That's just my estimate, not an official statistic. However, it is a known fact thus far that, women make up more of the body of Christ by a wide margin. Of course women would welcome the change if it were to occur. These women in the church have come from diverse cultures, backgrounds, histories, failures, successes, exposures, freedoms and boundaries, shapes and sizes, heights and colors, personalities, hurts and pains, disappointments and wounds, sufferings and injustices, and etc.... They have endeavored to become one with the body of Christ. Nevertheless, despite all the diversities, God has set the standard for virtuousness.

The standard God has given us is represented by "The Virtuous Woman" modeled in Proverbs Chapter 31. There is a small portion of women who have lived exemplary lives and have received favor in the sight of God and man. They are like the ones who finished school, taught Sunday School, remained virgins until marriage, stay married to one man until death do them apart, and so on... This truly is a very great achievement in a promiscuous world such as we live. However, they may also be the ones, who cannot understand how others can fall into such horrible, sin sick situations, and ones who do not have the compassion it takes to nurture others to spiritual healing and deliverance.

There are some women who have a few spots and wrinkles. They may be the ones who had a baby out of wedlock, but married and went on to finish school and to get decent jobs.

There are those who gathered around the wrong crowd of people and managed to escape the numbing sting of sin's consequences (drug addictions, alcoholism, prostitution, theft, jail and etc.). They found Jesus just in time.

Finally, there are those women who feel they have miserably failed God's standards. Some may have been in jail, or even prison. Some have been either addicted to drugs, sexually abused, school dropouts, promiscuous, mothers out of wedlock; or just plain envious and jealous hearted towards other sisters, etc. However, women who have faced these kinds of circumstances, when converted to Christianity, are not afraid to become soul winners for the Kingdom of God.

Yet, all of these women who have come into the knowledge of Jesus Christ and have something in common, and that is, a desire to continue the race and to press towards the mark of the high call to become a virtuous woman. However, problems arise within all the diversities. Many have been seeing and trying to obtain God's standard through man's eyes and their own understanding of what a virtuous woman is. Many of us have not been able to recognize through the Word of God, the Virtuous Woman's character in our own uniqueness. Nevertheless, we can be confident knowing that through God's eyes, we are virtuous. **"For my thoughts are not your thoughts, neither are your ways my ways, saith the Lord" (Isa. 55:8).** The Lord wants to make his ways known unto us.

Keep in mind that we (mankind) have inflated the personalities and personal backgrounds of biblical heroes to perfection, as pertaining to moral and social standings. We tend to focus more on those deemed "exceptional" characters of the Bible, instead of, focusing on the world of characters displayed in the Word.

We should examine the individual witness of Bible characters and their testimonies of overcoming the enemy; their deliverance, and their significant contributions to righteousness and the institution of God's divine plan of salvation for mankind. The scriptures carefully display the very realness of every man's life. The realness of their life includes their good and bad, their ups and downs, and their successes and failures, while showing us how to overcome the obstacles of life's trials. It is true that you cannot walk as a virtuous woman unless you choose to be saved and walk as a born-again believer. The moment you are saved, is the moment you have chosen to yield yourself to the divine destiny of

God's plan for your life. God then begins to put His Word in you and make you a new creature (Heb.10:16-17; 2 Cor. 5:17). It's true! God saw each of His children right where they were and still accomplished His divine will in their lives. God even displays His love towards each of His daughters by memorializing woman's ability to overcome the enemy in their lives through the examples and commendations in His Word.

Now, let us examine the standard God has given us for the Virtuous Woman modeled by Proverbs 31 by exploring the biographies of women portrayed throughout the scriptures. The principles of this book, "Portraits of A Virtuous Woman," are founded upon the inspirational scripture;

"Many daughters have done virtuously, but thou excellest them all."
Proverbs 31:29

Next, you will find this scripture translated in four different versions of the bible: KJV, NIV, Amplified and The Message. We will refer to the entire 31st Chapter of Proverbs throughout the course of this book, as these scriptures relate to the character of the women portrayed herein. Hopefully, you will get a clear understanding of this passage of scriptures, and be able to see your own virtuous portrait being perfected in the purpose of God for your life.

Proverbs 31:29

"Many daughters have done virtuously, but thou excellest them all."(KJV)

"Many women do noble things, but you surpass them all." (NIV)

"Many daughters have done virtuously, nobly, and well [with the strength of character that is steadfast in goodness], but you excel them all." (AMP)

"Many women have done wonderful things, but you've outclassed them all! "(The Message)

When I read this scripture, it leaped in my spirit. It was a "Right Now" word to encourage the purpose of my life. I knew I was called by God to accomplish great things, but in my limited and present state of being, I needed God to confirm again His unique commission for my life. As I read this scripture, I heard in my spirit three definite and complete confirmations to the daughters of God who would do even greater things than the women before them. God delighted to make honorable mention of these women in His Word.

The first thing I heard was **"many daughters"**. Not one, not two, not only the pure, not only the royal women, not only the Jewish women, but God said, **"many daughters"**. This includes women who are highly favored like Mary, the mother of our Savior (Luke 1:27-33). This includes women like Mary Magdalene from whom seven demons went out of, and yet, she was the first to see Jesus after His resurrection (John 20:1-18). This includes women like Rizpah, whose sufferings are at first ignored, but who refused to allow her sons to die in dishonor because of another man's vengeance (II Sam. 21:8- 14). This also includes women like the woman from Canaan who needed deliverance for her daughter, but was not a part of the Kingdom of God already. She humbled herself to receive from God, salvation for herself and her daughter (Matt. 15:22-28). Certainly, as we glance at these few women mentioned as an example, we can see that the scriptures are loaded with many daughters and those daughters are not limited to a certain upbringing or historical experiences, lifestyles, or ethnicity. God considered all of them to be His daughters. We, too, are considered to be God's daughters. It really does not matter where you come from, what you did, what ethnicity you are, rich, poor, etc... Do you get the picture yet? Upon giving your life to Christ, you too are considered a daughter of God's.

The second thing I heard was **"have done virtuously"** (KJV), **"do noble things"** (NIV), **"have done virtuously, nobly, and well"** (AMP), and **"have done wonderful things"** (The Message Bible). The Message of this honor and praise report from the daughters of God can be interpreted as: These women were, at some point in their life, able to comprehend, embrace, and display visible characteristics of proper and good moral and ethical conduct as becoming to that of a virtuous woman measured by God. All of the women thus far mentioned came to the crossroad of choice. There, these women allowed: God's Spirit of conviction in righteousness (Mary, the mother of our Saviour); God's hand of deliverance (Mary Magdalene); His Spirit of comfort and vindication (Rizpah); and God's healing virtue (Woman of Canaan) to have an opportunity in their lives and submitted to the divine plan of God for their life. That plan was for them to be recipients of an abundant life and for them to be used as an example of God's grace and mercy, showing forth His praise and glory. God desires that every woman will allow Him the opportunity to bestow the same manner of honor into and upon them with an even greater promise added to their

47

lives. There is only one difference in God's daughters today from those of yesterday, but the significance of the difference is great. Let's look at the next phrase of this verse.

Thirdly, I heard, **"but thou excellest them all" (KJV& AMP), "but you surpass them all" (NIV), "but you've outclassed them all!"** The Message reveals -- What is the difference? What would make us today, as daughters of God, excel, surpass, do more nobly, and out class them all? There is only one answer, "The Holy Spirit" living on the inside of us enabling us to do His good will and pleasure (Phil. 2:13). Prior to the promise of the Holy Spirit coming to live on the inside of us to empower us, victory over personal and corporate struggles depended upon the temporary move of the Holy Spirit within the atmosphere outside of man. Therefore, religious ceremonies demanded certain physical and mental activities be performed. These ceremonies would invoke the favor or punishment of God in a given situation. A woman accused of adultery by her husband had to submit to a ritual to prove whether or not she was guilty (Num. 5:13-31).

In other situations, the Holy Spirit would come upon them as He did with the mother of Jesus when, she was impregnated by His overshadowing her. They also had to reach out in obedience and touch something symbolic to receive their blessing as did the widow, when she baked the first cake for the prophet Elijah and her cruse of oil did not fail (I Kings 17:9-24). Even when God spoke clearly through a woman regarding spiritual things during this era, her voice was not heeded. Look at the wife of Pilate,

When he was set down on the judgment seat, his wife sent unto him, saying, Have thou nothing to do with that just man: for I have suffered many things this day in a dream because of him. Matthew 27:19

Pilate failed to pay attention to the righteous cry of his wife. She ran to him with urgency in her voice to keep him from killing a just man. Pilate chose his own counsel to manipulate the people's choice, hoping that they would make a common sense choice and free Jesus. The end resulted with the people saying, **Let him be crucified...** and innocent blood was shed (Matt. 27:20-24). Pilate's wife did virtuously. She obeyed God's instruction to intervene on the behalf of the divine unveiling of truth and righteousness presented to her in a dream. She is honorably mentioned in the scripture, but her voice was not adhered to. You, on the other hand, God's daughters have found favor by His Spirit and shall excel them all.

It was prophesied under the law that God's Spirit would do greater things in you, His daughters. Joel 2:28 – 29 says:

And it shall come to pass afterward, that I will pour out my spirit upon all flesh; and your sons and your daughters shall prophesy, your old men shall dream dreams, your young men shall see visions: (v29) And also upon the servants and upon the handmaids in those days will I pour out my spirit.

Whereas before, even if God spoke to His daughters, the traditions and laws of the time most often kept them from excelling. However, this prophecy was fulfilled on the Day of Pentecost and Peter boldly declared that Joel's prophecy was fulfilled (Acts 2:16-18). No law, no tradition, and no ceremony can stop the Holy Spirit from boldly getting the glory out of your life. Now as Proverbs 31 declares, your husband will trust you and praise you and your children will call you blessed. Strength and honor will be the command of your continence (paraphrased). This does not mean that you are perfect, or you had a perfect past life but the Holy Spirit is now residing in you, or wants to reside in you for a greater and more abundant life. The Lord, by His Spirit, will give you His beauty for your ashes and cause you to be a life giver in all areas of life (Isa. 61:13). A life that nurtures the life of others with great compassion is the principle of Proverbs 31.

Consider who wrote the Proverbs 31 and who it was written about. It was written by King Lemuel in remembrance of his mother's exhortation. She encourages him to stay away from women who destroy kings. This same king is rumored to be King Solomon. If this is truly a writing of King Solomon, then his mother would be none other than Bathsheba, the wife of King David who, because of sin, the death of her first husband and first son occurred. Even if this proverb was not written by King Solomon, King Lemuel makes it clear that his mother made and kept her vow to the Lord which spoke words of life to her son. This proverb is still profitable today. The Message Bible interpretation is: Every part of scripture is God-breathed and useful one way or another showing us truth, exposing our rebellion, correcting our mistakes, training us to live God's way. Through the Word we are put together and shaped up for the tasks God has for us. II Tim. 3:16-17

This is certainly true of the Proverbs 31 modeled wife and mother. However, God never restricted virtuosity in a woman to these verses of scripture in the Bible, no more than man being restricted to pray the Our Father's prayer modeled in Matthews 6, in order to pray appropriately and reach heaven. In fact, Jesus instructed us not to use "vain repetitions" (Matt. 6:7), but instead to pray after the manner of the model prayer. This prayer was the beginning of prayer in the right manner until they were baptized with the Holy Ghost.

Jesus knew it would take much more prayer than the model itself to take care of some of our spiritual needs and situations. For instance, Jude 21 tells us to build ourselves up on our most holy faith by praying in the Holy Ghost. According to Romans 8:26-27, we don't know what to pray and to avoid vain repetitions. The Spirit of God helps us so that the will of God will come forth in our lives. **The Message Bible reads this way:**

"Meanwhile, the moment we get tired in the waiting, God's spirit is right alongside helping us along. If we don't know how or what to pray, it doesn't matter. He [Sir Holy Spirit] does our praying in and for us, making prayer out of our wordless sighs, our aching groans. He knows us far better than we know ourselves, knows our pregnant condition, and keeps us present before God. That is why we can be so sure that every detail in our lives of love for God is worked into something good."

Likewise, virtuousness is not restricted to the model of the Proverbs 31 virtuous woman. We cannot crystallize the grace of God and limit His Word to our views. A king, who was encouraged by his mother to seek after a wife of such character, wrote the point of view in the 31st Chapter of Proverbs. But, because every individual is unique and brings to the Body of Christ specific gifts, cultural up-bringing, diversified histories and legacies, and resources, the Word is much broader in the perfecting of the saints.

Women have been mentioned over and over again, in regards to their gifts, talents and character as memorials to their contributions to the spreading of the Gospel. Journey with me now to examine just a few Portraits of Virtuous Women divinely framed in the Word of God.

PORTRAIT ONE

"A Deceived and Seductive Woman"

EVE

Genesis 1:27-3

What was Eve's first moral state?

Eve is the only woman who has ever lived that could not say, **"Behold, I was shapen in iniquity and in sin did my mother conceive me"** (Ps. 51:5). This woman was uniquely designed. She was so unrepeatable and unlike any of God's other creations. God chose not to form her from the dust of the ground. Instead, He reached into His own earthly image, man, and pulled out a rib to form her, the first woman, Eve (Gen. 2:19, 21, 22). Perfected, not even the suspicion of sin came to her mind when, she was approached by Satan in the Garden of Eden. Why? Because God created them (Adam and Eve) in His own image. They only had knowledge of good (Gen. 1:27).

What was God's plan for her life?

God formed Eve, the first woman, with a uniquely ordained and divine purpose in mind. She was to be a companion and helper to her husband and the mother of all mankind (Gen. 2:23-25). Eve was to be an expression of God's extraordinary intimacy with mankind and His desire to produce life through an eternal covenant of love, sharing, and commitment to her husband and all creation. God taking a rib from Adam created a symbolism that Adam and Eve were both incomplete without each other. With the honor and joy of consummation between them, they became one and brought forth life (Gen. 1:28). The Greek word for the two of them becoming one is "echad", which means- "collect and unite together and be complete." Nothing was to hinder, interfere, or interrupt this divine unity and symbolic covenant relationship (Gen. 2:24, Matt. 19:6).

The design of Adam and Eve's intimate relationship represented God's love towards and intimacy with His Bride (the Church), a holy and set apart people. Adam and Eve were so holy, that God could enjoy visiting them in the Garden of Eden just for fellowship, as you and I do when we delight to visit friends (Gen. 3:8). God pronounced a blessing over Adam and Eve for them to reproduce and their seed would cover the entire earth (Gen.1:28). Communion with God impregnated them with God's vision and purpose for their lives. Adam and Eve could not have children without coming together spiritually, mentally, and physically. Intimacy was an adventure for them. Their affections received each other. They delighted to explore each other, and they were passionate about expressing their pleasure being with one another. A seed of life was planted within Eve, **"Adam knew Eve his wife, and she conceived, and bare Cain"** (Gen. 4:1). She did bring forth life.

What was her sin?

All of creation knows that despite her perfection, purpose, and blessings, the first woman who was given the name, Eve was deceived into sin. That sin caused her to seduce her husband into sin, thereby corrupting their lives and the whole creation (Gen. 3:1-7)

> (v1) Now the serpent was more subtle than any beast of the field which the Lord God had made. And he said unto the woman, Yea, hath God said, Ye shall not eat of every tree of the garden? (v2) And the woman said unto the serpent, We may eat of the fruit of the trees of the garden: (v3) But of the fruit of the tree which is in the midst of the garden, God hath said, Ye shall not eat of it, neither shall ye touch it, lest ye die. (v4) And the serpent said unto the woman, Ye shall not surely die: (v5) For God doth know that in the day ye eat thereof, then your eyes shall be opened, and ye shall be as gods, knowing good and evil. (v6) And when the woman saw that the tree was good for food, and that it was pleasant to the eyes, and a tree to be desired to make one wise, she took of the fruit thereof, and did eat, and gave also unto her husband with her; and he did eat. (v7) And the eyes of them both were opened, and they knew that they were naked; and they sewed fig leaves together, and made themselves aprons.

There was an enemy present that day in the garden to destroy the God in Adam by using his wife, Eve. The devil, through the serpent, took notice of how awestruck Eve was about the garden's contents. Perhaps Satan observed Eve's attitude while exploring and discovering all of life's resources in the garden with such amazement. Maybe, he further noticed that Adam trusted Eve to choose the fruit of the day. It is possible that Satan observed Eve feeding Adam grapes, strawberries, or melon out of the palm of her hands. Or could it have been the expression of joy on each of their faces as they romantically teased each other while eating.

Somehow, the devil noticed that the only thing Adam was more enchanted with in the garden was the woman that God made from his bone. He enjoyed everything else but not more than he enjoyed woman. Adam was proud to admit, **This is now bone of my bones, and flesh of my flesh...** I'm going to call her "woman" because she is the rib that makes me whole (Gen. 2:24). After observing what Adam was most vulnerable to, the serpent approached Eve. It has often been said that Adam was not close to where Eve was at the time all of this was going on. But, the scripture says in verse 6 that Eve, **took of the fruit thereof, and did eat, and gave also unto her husband "with" her; and he did eat.**

Nevertheless, in her usual manner, because her eyes were not yet open, she proceeded to feed her husband from the palm of her hands. Then, verse 7 says, **"the eyes of them both were opened.** "They were standing there with no clothes on and they discovered that they were **"naked"**. Not just physically, but naked of the Holy Spirit within them, who protected them from the flood of evils that lurked around them, had now started dimming as darkness started creeping in.

What kind of guilt and shame did she experience?

One day while I was meditating on Eve's life and asking questions of the Lord regarding some of the injustices against women in the Bible and life itself, the Lord ministered revelation to me regarding Eve and the life of His daughters. As I was sitting at a table, the Holy Spirit within me began to weep as I read this part of Eve's story (Gen. 3:9-13)

> And the Lord God called unto Adam, and said unto him, Where art thou? (v10) And he said, I heard thy voice in the garden, and I was afraid, because I was naked; and I hid myself. (v11) And he said, Who told thee that thou wast naked? Hast thou eaten of the tree, whereof I commanded thee that thou shouldest not eat? (v12) And the man said, The woman whom thou gavest to be with me, she gave me of the tree, and I did eat. (v13) And the Lord God said unto the woman, What is this that thou hast done? And the woman said, The serpent beguiled me, and I did eat.
>
> God spoke to my spirit very dearly and said, "I'M SORRY" to all women that day. Well, what happened? Why did God say, "I'M SORRY" ? It is right within verse "13".

And the Lord God said unto the woman, what is this that thou hast done?

Allow yourself to envision Eve in the Garden of Eden on that day. It was the most horrible day of her life. For the first time, after her eyes were opened, she felt sin. She went from holy to sinful within seconds. There she stood naked with no peace, no comfort, and no rest because sin had taken a grip on her life. Can you imagine how I felt running from the stage that day when the cameras came into the club to take pictures of my almost nude body to expose them to the whole world? Think of your most embarrassing moment on the face of the earth. Embarrassment is a tormenting experience. Eve's day was worse than any embarrassment that we have ever experienced.

Eve knew that her once innocent, playful enticing of her husband had become seduction instead of sharing. Now man had fallen to sin. When the Holy, Immortal, Almighty, and All Powerful God came to the garden and called them to His presence, Eve stood naked between God and her husband. She then heard her husband blame her saying, **"The woman whom thou gavest to be with me, she gave me of the tree, and I did eat**." Suddenly, God turned and looked at, Eve, and said, **"What is this that thou has done?"** Imagine Eve that day standing between a Holy God whose appearance makes sin bow down and her husband, Adam, who once found no fault in her. She knew from now on when he would look at her, he would remember what they had in the garden and lost because of her weakness and seductiveness. Although Adam once looked at Eve and called her bone of my bone with a consuming love, she knew now, every time the garden yielded thorns and thistles (Gen. 3:18), he would look at her with contempt. Just hearing this Holy God say those words to her and her husband blaming her for everything, must have given her a sense of worthlessness.

What was the punishment and how was she punished?

God said to the woman, **I will greatly multiply thy sorrow and thy conception; in sorrow thou shalt bring forth children; and thy desires shall be to thy husband, and he shall rule over**

thee (Gen. 3:16). Eve was "woman" before she was Eve. Woman was the name of the nations of women that would come from her seed perpetually through all generations. Therefore, her womanly sorrows began with her personal life as Eve and continued throughout generations of her seed as woman.

Given over to Adam's lordship, **thy desires shall be to thy husband, and he shall rule over thee**, her tears greatly multiplied. For with this rule, man hardened his heart against the woman and abused the principles of the marriage relationship (Gen. 2:24; Matt. 19:7-8; Eph. 5:29-33). Eve and every woman under the law was considered to be greatly inferior, rebellious, and the property of man with no true identity or rights. It even came to pass that men had multiple wives. An example is King Solomon who had 700 wives and 300 concubines who were inferior-common law wives (I King 11:3). In addition, a wife could be divorced if she no longer appealed to her husband (Deut. 24:1). And, a wife and her children could be sold to pay debts (Neh. 5:4-5; Amos 2:6-7; 8:6).

It is possible that on the day that Eve sinned, her spirit was filled with feelings of rejection, insecurities, inferiority, depression, resentfulness, anger, and jealousy – all of which she would later breed into her children. We can see signs of these emotions through her first two sons, Cain and Able. One brother killed the other because God rejected his personal character (Gen. 4:5-8). There in the garden that day, as a woman, Eve's voice was silenced. Her image was made insignificant, and her womanhood ignored. She became the living dead. Living because she did feel, she did hear, she did care and she was alive. She had thoughts, concerns, opinions, and contributions that mattered. Dead because she was, at first, at the mercy of man, who had denied his contribution to their fallen estate and denied her worth.

Eve was punished that day, but a great thing happened to her, she received a proclamation from God that said, **I will put enmity between thee and the woman, and between thy seed and her seed; it shall bruise thy head, and thou shalt bruise his heel** (Gen. 3:15). Although Satan had caused the fall of man and would continue his oppression, he (the serpent) would be **cursed above all cattle, and above every beast of the field** (Gen. 3:14). God made sure that the woman would now become his enemy with deep-seated hatred in her heart for him. She would teach her seed of Satan's deadly venom and her teachings would cause her seed to crush Satan's head. Thus, preventing their utter death and reinforcing their dominion over Satan and sin.

Why did God allow all of Eve's (woman's) sufferings?

God was angry with the woman and hid his face from her. He looked at Eve's seduction just as He did when men became so wicked on the earth that He flooded the earth,

> (v5) And God saw that the wickedness of man was great in the earth, and that every imagination of the thoughts of his heart was only evil continually. (v6) And it repented the Lord that he had made man on the earth, and it grieved him at his heart. Gen. 6:5-6

See how God compares them,

> (v6) For the Lord hath called thee as a woman forsaken and grieved in spirit, and a wife of youth, when thou wast refused, saith thy God. (v7)For a small moment have I forsaken thee; but with great mercies will I gather thee. (v8) In a little wrath I hid my face from thee for a moment; but with everlasting

kindness will I have mercy on thee, saith the Lord thy Redeemer. (v9) For this is as the waters of Noah unto me: for as I have sworn that the waters of Noah should no more go over the earth; so have I sworn that I would not be wroth with thee, nor rebuke thee. Isa. 54:6-9

What is God's promise to us that is being fulfilled by His Spirit?

Read the following;

> (v10) For the mountains shall depart, and the hills be removed; but my kindness shall not depart from thee, neither shall the covenant of my peace be removed, saith the Lord that hath mercy on thee. (v11) O thou afflicted, tossed with tempest, and not comforted, behold, I will lay thy stones with fair colors, and lay thy foundations with sapphires. (v12) And I will make thy windows of agates, and thy gates of carbuncles, and all thy borders of pleasant stones. (v13) And all thy children shall be taught of the Lord; and great shall be the peace of thy children. (v14) In righteousness shalt thou be established: thou shalt be far from oppression for thou shalt not fear: and from terror; for it shall not come near thee. (v15) Behold, they shall surely gather together, but not by me: whosoever shall gather together against thee shall fall for thy sake. (v16) Behold, I have created the smith that bloweth the coals in the fire, and that bringeth forth an instrument for his work; and I have created the waster to destroy. (v17) No weapon that is formed against thee shall prosper; and every tongue that shall rise against thee in judgment thou shalt

condemn. This is the heritage of the servants of the Lord, and their righteousness is of me, saith the Lord. Isa. 54:10-17

Men and women alike are always making mockery of Eve's deception. However, the bold and astounding truth is, "Eve received every one of these blessings and so do we!" God stepped right in to provide her with the assurance she needed that her seed would be able to destroy the demonic forces that would try to take their life (Gen. 3:15). Eve confessed her sin before God (Gen. 3:13), and God was faithful and just to cover her sins (Gen. 3:21). She was still Adam's helper and wife. She still became the mother of all mankind and she still expressed through her seed, God's extraordinary covenant of intimacy with His Bride-The Church. Eve endured hardships and continued to bless and acknowledge God in all of her ways (Gen. 4:1, 25). We can especially appreciate the fact that "no weapon" prospered to the destruction of her purpose and "every tongue" that has risen up against her can be condemned. Nothing could hinder her from fulfilling the call of God on her life, not even a deceitful or seductive reputation.

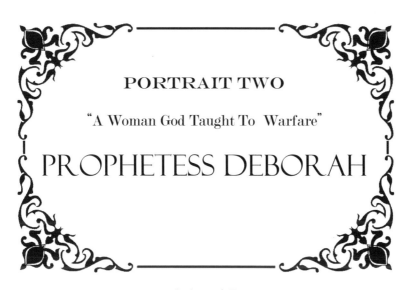

"A Woman God Taught To Warfare"

PROPHETESS DEBORAH

Judges 4-5

Where did she come from and was there sin in her life?

Glancing into the life of the Prophetess Deborah, we have no details of her upbringing, education, family history, or marriage, except that the name of her husband was Lapidoth. Scriptures do not reveal to us how she came to be a voice for God in judging Israel. She was unlike the Prophetess Miriam, who was found with fault of murmuring against her brother Moses, the servant of God. Miriam was exiled for seven days from among the people of God and plagued with leprosy for her sin. She was later restored to her position, a prophetess among the people (Num. 12:1-15). We cannot collect any faults found in the Prophetess Deborah's character prior to or concluding her ministry in scripture. There is, meanwhile, a great deal of wise insight and encouragement for women to be seen in the virtuous image of Prophetess Deborah.

What vulnerabilities did she have to overcome and what was her character like?

We find Prophetess Deborah's life an extraordinary exception to the period of time in which she lived. She was a woman who would make a significant contribution to the Kingdom of God. There were several distinct obstacles that could have been a crippling factor to her performing the Call of God on her life but her exceptional faith was triumphant.

First, her prophetic calling was during a time that Israel had been **mightily oppressed** for **twenty years** (Jud. 4:4). She was to confirm Barak's vision from God to go to war. After encountering a stronghold over and over again, and enduring it year after year, after year, one's faith may become wavering. Many times we desire to endure and keep going, while hoping for God's salvation and deliverance from whatever bondage is present. We keep asking God to show up. But, oftentimes our expectancy just turns to wishing that our petition would come to pass without the conviction in our heart to sustain our confidence. This is what happened to Barak when Deborah confronted him with God's charge to lead Israel to victory in war against King Jabin of Canaan:

> "And Barak said unto her, if thou wilt go with me, then I will go: but if thou wilt not go with me, then I will not go." Judges 4:8

Barak heard the voice of God, but his belief turned into unbelief. He rehearsed time and time again in his mind the scene of King Jabin's **nine hundred chariots of iron** and the last **twenty years** of their strongholds over Israel. He needed his faith to be reinforced and Deborah was the person to do it! Even though

Deborah had experienced the same twenty years of oppression, her faith was unshaken. Look at her reply,

> And she said, I will surely go with thee: notwithstanding the journey that thou takest shall not be for thine honour; for the Lord shall sell Sisera into the hand of a woman. And Deborah arose, and went with Barak to Kedesh. Judges 4:9

Secondly, Deborah was a married woman.

> And Deborah, a prophetess, the wife of Lapidoth, she judged Israel at that time. Judges 4:4

As a married woman in those days, all of her virtuous and noble services should have been devoted to pleasing her husband and serving her family. Any open vows to the Lord that she made, while married or unmarried, could have been **disallowed** by her husband, Lapidoth. The following law granted him this authority: (v6) And if she had at all an husband, when she vowed, or uttered ought out of her lips, wherewith she bound her soul; (v7) And her husband heard it, and held his peace at her in the day that he heard it: then her vows shall stand, and her bonds wherewith she bound her soul shall stand. (v8) But if her husband disallowed her on the day that he heard it; then he shall make her vow which she vowed, and that which she uttered with her lips, wherewith she bound her soul, of none effect: and the Lord shall forgive her. Num. 30:6-8

Some scholars believe that Deborah was a very dominant woman, who was the head of her household in every aspect but Proverbs 31 indicates differently. Certainly, she was able **to judge righteously (v9); her husband safely trusted in her (v11); and her husband was known in the gates among the elders** of the land (v23). There are other characteristics in Proverbs 31 that would describe Deborah's well known nobility we will not mention but we can truly see why her husband, Lapidoth would not disallow her vows to God before man.

The third and last obstacle to be viewed is Prophetess Deborah was a judge who did not have an official throne to sit on or tabernacle in which to judge. How this woman came to the position of "judging all of Israel" still remains a mystery. We do know, however, that wise and devout men were chosen by Moses to officially be judges over the concerns of God's people (Ex. 18:21-26). See also the following verses:

> (v16) And the Lord said unto Moses, Gather unto me seventy men of the elders of Israel, whom thou knowest to be the elders of the people, and officers over them; and bring them unto the tabernacle of the congregation, that they may stand there with thee. (v17) And I will come down and talk with thee there: and I will take of the spirit which is upon thee, and will put it upon them; and they shall bear the burden of the people with thee, that thou bear it not thyself alone. Num. 11:16-17

Somehow, through Deborah's endurance of twenty years of oppression, being a married woman, and her living in a time that it was considered to be a man's world, God brought forth the Prophetess Deborah into her divine destiny.

What was Deborah's calling in life and did she fulfill it?

Deborah wore, as it has been said, many hats. She is a prime example of being such a faithful and wise steward over her talents that God would make her ruler over much (Luke 12:42-44). She was first called to be a wife to Lapidoth (Judges 4:4). One could only imagine her to be a wife that knew how to please her husband as Paul indicated a wife should (I Cor. 7:34). It would be hard to believe that she enforced a dominant rule over her husband with a man like Barak, a leading ruler of Israel, who was pleased to come to her and be led by her wise counsel to war. Her noble character reminded him that the victory would go to a woman but he did not reconsider his decision. Deborah remained married, so we can safely reason that she pleased both God and her man. Thereby, God increased her talents.

Secondly, we notice that God presents this wife with the gift of a word of knowledge and wisdom. We have noted only one event in the Word of Deborah's wisdom and true ability to provide counseling but what a powerful example it is:

> (v6) And she sent and called Barak the son of Abinoam out of Kedesh-naphtali, and said unto him, Hath not the Lord God of Israel commanded, saying, Go and draw toward mount Tabor, and take with thee ten thousand men of the children of Naphtali and of the children of Zebulun? (v7) And I will draw unto thee to the river Kishon Sisera, the captain of Jabin's army, with his chariots and his multitude; and I will deliver him into thine hand. Judge 4:6-7

In this documentation of Deborah's life, we find that the Spirit of the Lord rested upon her as Isaiah described it would rest upon Jesus (Isa. 11:2). She received revelation, visions of the future, and failed not to cry out God's direction in the wilderness for her people. Boldly, she sent forth a word of knowledge, wisdom, and counsel to Barak that would save all Israel from its twenty years of oppression. Interwoven in all of this, we again see another talent.

We find thirdly, in the fibers of Deborah's portrait, her ability to judge with the gift of prophecy. Deborah not only judged all Israel

(Jud. 4:4), but she also judged Barak's fear of the enemy and his disbelief in God's assistance to win the war. She prophesied that a woman would be able to claim the honor of the battle's victory (Jud. 4:9). Late in the battle, at the very end of the battle, a woman by the name of Jael killed Sisera, the captain of the enemy's army:

> Then Jael Heber's wife took a nail of the tent, and took an hammer in her hand, and went softly unto him, and smote the nail into his temples, and fastened it into the ground: for he was fast asleep and weary. So he died. Judges 4:21

Deborah's judgment and prophecy came true, right at the end of the battle when all the men of the nine hundred chariots of iron were already dead. Barak chased after Sisera to the end in order to say that he conquered all but the true prophecy of Deborah's lips failed not.

The forth gift of the Prophetess Deborah sums up her whole life -- the grand finale, as we say. God taught this woman "WARFARE" throughout her life and through twenty years of oppression. God then makes her commander of His army, Israel! Just as Deborah is believed to have been an honorable wife, yet wiser than her husband to judge all Israel, the same sentiments were expressed in her relationship with Barak.

Barak was chosen by God to defeat the army of King Jabin. He had received instructions personally from God but fainted with fear of failure and the possibility of death. It was revealed to the prophetess by God that He had already spoken to Barak, **"Hath not the Lord God of Israel commanded"** (Jud. 4:6). Accordingly, the Prophetess Deborah sent word to him confirming God's word (Deut.19:15) and encouraged his obedience. Barak, however, placed the responsibility back on the shoulders of Deborah:

And Barak said unto her, If thou wilt go with me, then I will go: but if thou wilt not go with me, then I will not go. (Jud. 4:8)

God did not tell her to go. But, Deborah was not about to let the oppression continue when God in essence said, I've heard the prayers of my people and the time has come that I will give your enemy over into your hands. She replied, **"I will surely go with thee"** (Jud. 4:9), and she did go. It was Deborah who gave the final instructions to go to war.

(v14) And Deborah said unto Barak, Up; for this is the day in which the Lord hath delivered Sisera into thine hand: is not the Lord gone out before thee? So Barak went down from mount Tabor, and ten thousand men after him. (v15) And the Lord discomfited Sisera, and all his chariots, and all his host, with the edge of the sword before Barak; so that Sisera lighted down off his chariot, and fled away on his feet. (v16) But Barak pursued after the chariots, and after the host, unto Harosheth of the Gentiles: and all the host of Sisera fell upon the edge of the sword; and there was not a man left. Judges 4:14-16

Deborah ends the battle with a victory song. Within the song, she refers to herself as a mother who rose in Israel. Godly mothers love their children so much; they would give their life in defending them. Deborah had a mother's love for Israel (Judges 5:7). The war ended in celebration with Deborah, the wife, prophetess, judge, and warrior leader singing praises unto God for his mighty acts. What an extraordinary portrait of Deborah who fulfilled her calling victoriously! Can you relate to the burdens of ministry in this woman's life? Yet, God's grace was sufficient and she made it through to the end of her oppression.

"The Harlot Who Had a Scarlet Thread Salvation"
RAHAB AKA RACHAB

Joshua 2:1-21; 6:16-17, 22-25; Matt. 1:5-17

Who was this woman?

"And Joshua the son of Nun sent out of Shittim two men to spy secretly, saying, Go view the land, even Jericho. And they went, and came into an harlot's house, named Rahab, and lodged there." Joshua 2:1

WOW! What a way to introduce one of the great..., grandmothers of Jesus Christ. She is first known in the scripture as a "harlot", a whore, a prostitute, being interpreted as, a woman who sold her body. Those words don't read so nice or sound too pleasant to hear when said, do they? If I were to be a guest speaker, witnessing on the behalf of God's deliverance in my life, I certainly would not want to be introduced to the Church as the Harlot, Evangelist Cynthia Carter. You and I would try to pretend that no such character existed in our lives, ever! However, there is an extraordinary display of God's love and commitment to bless sinners who recognize Him as, **God in heaven above, and in earth beneath** (Joshua 2:11); and to those who want to be saved.

71

Rahab did both. She recognized Him as Lord and she wanted Him to save her. As a result, she was included in the main genetic family line of the great grandmothers of Jesus Christ. She gave birth to Booz (the same as Boaz) and Booz married Ruth. Ruth gave birth to Jessie who was the father of King David... and right on down the line to the birth of Jesus Christ (Matt. 1:5-16). After taking a look into Rahab's portrait, no woman should feel that she cannot be accepted or used by God because of a past life that demeaned their character.

How did she become a harlot and what were her struggles?

In Israel's culture, the scripture offers us a few reasons why young women and even some wives ended up into harlotry to support their livelihood. Parents sometimes imposed the life sentence of a harlot upon their daughters (Lev. 19:29); and women who experienced marital breakup or the death of their husband, in the Old Testament, often resulted to harlotry for survival (Lev. 21:7, 14). Regardless of the reason that an Israelite woman would come to this particular lifestyle, neither she or her money was allowed in the temple (Deut. 23:18). Nor was she permitted to marry any man that was in a covenant with God (Lev. 21:14). There were no means to free this type of character from sin.

In Rahab's culture, there were no penalties existing or executed by the king or the people against harlotry on the behalf of their god. In fact, there are four types of harlotry mentioned in Bible, one of the four being normal prostitution where sexual intercourse was exchanged for money. Another of the four would be cult prostitution (Hos. 4:14). This type of prostitution is associated with heathen worship unto their god in hopes that their god would also engage in sexual conduct to cause their land, cattle, and families to be reproductive and plenteous. That is not to say that this is the type of harlotry Rahab engaged in. We can only speculate as to the reason why Rahab became a harlot in her heathen land, Jericho. What we do know is that Rahab was marked with this distinctive character. The King of Jericho and the town's people knew well of Rahab's harlotry and accepted her way of life indicated by the following scriptures,

> (v2) And it was told the king of Jericho, saying, Behold, there came men in hither to night of the children of Israel to search out the country. (v3) And the king of Jericho sent unto Rahab, saying, Bring forth the men that are come to thee, which are entered into thine house: for they come to search out all the country.   Joshua 2:2-3

Rehab was a young, single, and childless woman during the time period in which she lived as a harlot. She lived alone and appeared to fare well in prosperity, indicated by her possession of the scarlet thread that was strong enough to let men down through the window. The scarlet thread itself was expensive and represented a good and fashionable lifestyle. King Solomon dressed his wives with scarlet attire (II Sam. 1:24). Despite the fact that she had no husband or children, Rahab expressed a great deal of love and concern for the safety of her father's house. She loved her family so much that when she was given the opportunity to be saved, she ask the two men of Israel to give their word of oath to include the safety of her father's house, before mentioning her own safety.

> (v12) Now therefore, I pray you, swear unto me by the Lord, since I have shewed you kindness, that ye will also shew kindness unto my father's house, and give me a true token: (v13) And that ye will save alive my father, and my mother, and my brethren, and my

73

sisters, and all that they have, and deliver our lives from death. Joshua 2:12-13

Rahab had considered and pondered in her heart, all of the stories told to her and discussed among her people about Israel and their God. She admitted that the consciousness of their presence in their land brought an immobilizing and taunting fear to even the men of her city.

> (v9) And she said unto the men, I know that the Lord hath given you the land, and that your terror is fallen upon us, and that all the inhabitants of the land faint because of you. (v10) For we have heard how the Lord dried up the water of the Red sea for you, when ye came out of Egypt; and what ye did unto the two kings of the Amorites, that were on the other side Jordan, Sihon and Og, whom ye utterly destroyed. (v11) And as soon as we had heard these things, our hearts did melt, neither did there remain any more courage in any man, because of you: for the Lord your God, he is God in heaven above, and in earth beneath. Joshua 2:9-11

Rahab was faced with a dilemma of believing that salvation was possible for all of her family. Although she and her family would be as heathens among the Israelites, she wanted their lives spared. What made her believe that she could be saved from the destruction that the previous nations had faced? In Sihon and Og all were killed, men, women, and children (Deut. 3:1-6). God did not shower any mercy upon them. Moreover, asking for the life of her family could have meant that they would come to the Israelites as prisoners of war and taken to be servants (Num. 31:7-9). But here, Rahab dares to confess and believe that the Israelites' God is not just the God of the Israelites. **He is God in heaven above,**

and in earth beneath! When she said this, she took the limits off of God saving only the Israelites and said within herself, "Surly He is God of both heaven and earth, He can be my God too. I want to know Him and live for Him if I have to be among a strange and a peculiar nation. So be it! Even if I have to learn a new way of life, He will become my God and I will become His servant. It is evident that His people are blessed and I want to be blessed too."

Rahab took notice that sudden destruction was coming upon her entire nation of people, all because of God's favor upon His people, the Israelites. She moved with a holy fear and respect for this God and His people. Rahab repented from her familiar lifestyle and denounced her nation. She forsook all to have the gift of God - "Life" - and to have Him control her destiny.

What did Rahab's divine future include?

Rahab received an extraordinary new life. Within days, she was delivered from a life sentence of heathen living and harlotry, to God bestowing an abundant new life with the people of God. He did not take away the knowledge of her past but destroyed the affliction of her past from ever again having a stronghold in her life. In this new life, she first received life for herself and all of her blood relatives that took heed to her voice of warning from the forth coming destruction (Jos. 6:22-23).

Secondly, as you remember reading earlier, harlots could not marry men of God among the Israelites. But here, God's mercy and grace showered down upon Rahab to the degree that it is obvious that she found favor in the sight of God and man. A man in covenant with God named Salom fell in love with Rahab and married her (Matt. 1:5).

Thirdly, I believe that Rahab's life sings a song to the words of Romans 5:8:

> But God commendeth his love towards us, in that, while we were yet sinners, Christ died for us.

Out of all the women in the nation of Israel who kept themselves from such a demoralizing character, or of all the women of the heathen nation of Jericho, who was not of such character; God chose this heathen, harlot Rahab. He blessed her newly found covenant marriage to Salom and opened her womb to conceive and bare a son, Boaz, the first fruit in her new life with God.

What a great man of God her son grew to be. God used Rahab also to further implement his progressive covenant of love, mercy, forgiveness, and salvation towards mankind by blessing her seed through generations until the birth of the Christ.

What was so virtuous about Rahab?

The first glimpse of virtuousness we can see in Rehab is that she heard the testimony of God's miracle working power in that He **dried up the waters of the Red sea** (2:10) and delivered nations unto the hands of His people. She was already convinced that the Lord is "The LORD".

> "And she said unto the men, I know that the Lord hath given you the land..." Joshua 2:9

> "Now, therefore, I pray you, swear unto me by the Lord..." Joshua 2:12

Rahab did not say, I know that your Lord gave you the land. Nor did she say, swear unto me by your Lord... She said, "**swear unto me by the Lord.**" Rahab talked as if her relationship with God revealed to her what was about to take place. Did she start praying to this God before the spies came to her home? Did God divinely reveal Himself to her and the purpose of the two men coming to her house? Did God instruct her not to reveal the whereabouts of the two men as He instructed the three wise men not to reveal the place where baby Jesus was (Matt. 2:12)? Had God revealed to her that salvation was coming to her house as He revealed to Cornelius, a man of another heathen nation, that Peter would declare salvation to him and his home with the following words?

> (v34) Then Peter opened his mouth, and said, Of a truth I perceive that God is no respector of persons: (v35) But in every nation he that feareth him, and worketh righteousness, is accepted with him. Act 10:34-35

In chapter 10 of the book of Acts, there are more details of Cornelius' and his household's acceptance into the lifestyle of Christianity. It certainly appears that Rahab had some understanding and insight into God's plan that was about to take place in the land. Therefore, she moved with fear and trembling to hide the men upon her roof prior to the king sending for them. God had already begun to establish her thoughts and to direct her in a new pathway of life.

Secondly, Rahab never looked back! Sometimes we agonize over abrupt changes that occur in our lives because they appear to be destructive to all of our hopes and dreams that we want to accomplish. We cannot always see how the end result is going to turn out. Lot's wife looked back longing to keep her present lifestyle when destruction came to her city. God was trying to save her family. As a result of looking back, she experienced the same death that the city experienced. The fire consumed her and turned her into a pillar of salt (Gen. 19:26). Not Rahab! She did not let the fear of future uncertainties prevent her from accepting this new life by faith. Rahab faces all of the challenges with grace! She did not wallow in self-pity, or say, "It's impossible for me to change my lifestyle." She never said, "My family couldn't be saved because of who I am or what I've done." Rather, she grabbed hold of salvation for both her family and herself.

Thirdly, Rahab moved to be a prophetic voice of salvation to her family. The Bible does not elaborate on the details of how she was able to convince her family of the destruction to come. Instead of **the heart of a husband trusting her**, she has a family that safely trusted in her with their heart so that there is no need for their spoil (Prov. 31:11).

Fourth and lastly, Rahab knew when to accept warning, when to ask for salvation, and when to trust in God's ability to give her a new life. It does not matter where we come from, where we have been, or what we have done. Nor does it matter who's fault it is that we are in the predicaments we are in because **all have sinned, and come short of the glory of God** (Ro. 3:23).

It "does matter" what choices we make when presented with the opportunity to change or come out of our sin. Rahab was very courageous in choosing her new life with God. The reward of her courage blossomed into an encouraging monument in the Word of God for the whole world to see how the scarlet thread represented the gift of her salvation.

Judges 4:17-23; 5:24-27

Who was Jael?

Jael was another woman used of God who was not an Israelite. She was the woman that God used to fulfill the prophecy of the Prophetess Deborah. She was also the wife of Heber,

> And she (Deborah) said, I will surely go with thee: notwithstanding the journey that thou takest shall not be for thine honor; for the Lord shall sell Sisera into the hand of a woman...Judges 4:9a

> Howbeit Sisera fled away on his feet to the tent of Jael the wife of Heber the Kenite: for there was peace between Jabin the king of Hazor and the house of Heber the Kenite. Judges 4:17

Jael may have considered herself to be only a wife to Heber but suddenly, out of nowhere, her divine destiny was presented. It was recorded of her the same words that was recorded and spoken of Mary, the mother of our Lord, Jesus the Christ.

> "Blessed above women shall Jael the wife of Heber the Kenite be, blessed shall she be above women in the tent." Judges 5:24

Look at what the angel said to Mary and compare the praise given of both women,

> "And the angel came in unto her, and said, Hail, thou that art highly favoured, the Lord is with thee: blessed art thou among women." Luke 1:28

What were Jael's struggles?

What an extraordinary example of being overtaken with a blessing (Deut. 28:2).

She was married to a Kenite man named Heber. The Kenite people were the relatives of Jethro, the father-in-law of Moses. Moses was a great deliver of God's people from their bondage under Pharaoh the king of Egypt. Their link to Moses gave the Kenites favor in the eyes of the Israelites and they befriended them for several generations (Jud. 1:16; 4:11). The Kenites enjoyed the same blessings of God as did the Israelites because of their relationship with God's people (Num. 10:29-32). But, there came a time when the Lord allowed King Jabin of Canaan to afflict and harass Israel with his rule for twenty years because of Israel's disobedience (Jud. 4:1-3).

During these twenty years of affliction, the word of God says that Jael's husband, Heber **severed himself from the**

Kenites (Jud. 4:11). He separated from them and became friendly or at **peace** with King Jabin (Jud. 4:17). Most of us have had friends who will leave us when we are down and out. As long as things were going well for Israel, Heber enjoyed the benefits of their friendship and their blessings. But as soon as another power and authority appeared to take over, Heber looked out for his own interest.

He moved away from Israel and betrayed them by befriending their enemy for survival. Jael on the other hand may have had to follow her husband but she remained committed within her heart to her relationship with the Israelites and their God.

What did Jael do to fulfill prophecy and was it honorable?

With some milk, a hammer, and a nail, Jael brought to an end the last representation of Israel's affliction under the reign of King Jabin by killing Sisera, the captain of his army.

> (v18) And Jael went out to meet Sisera, and said unto him, Turn in, my lord, turn in to me; fear not. And when he had turned in unto her into the tent, she covered him with a mantle. (v19) And he said unto her, Give me, I pray thee, a little water to drink; for I am thirsty. And she opened a bottle of milk, and gave him drink, and covered him. (v20) Again he said unto her, Stand in the door of the tent, and it shall be, when any man doth come and enquire of thee, and say, Is there any man here? that thou shalt say, No. (v21) Then Jael Heber's wife took a nail of the tent, and took an hammer in her hand, and went softly unto him, and smote the nail into his temples, and fastened it into the ground: for he was fast asleep and weary. So he died.

It is true, in this case, that enmity was between the serpent, (persecution of God's people) and the woman. Just as Eve, she would bruise the head of her enemy (Gen. 3:15). Some expository readings present Jael as an ill character and not befitting of a Godly woman because of the way she coaxed Sisera into her tent and killed him. Perhaps, this was because it was believed to be truly disgraceful to a man's honor, if they lost their life at the hands of a woman in battle. Another Bible reference to this belief is the woman who cast down a stone upon the head of King Abimelech and injured him to the point that death would occur. Before he died, he requested that his Armour-bearer kill him with a sword to prevent a woman from taking the credit of killing him (Jud. 9:52-54). Jael engaged in appropriate warfare just as the Prophetess Deborah and the woman who cast the stone down upon the head of king Abimelech. Comparably today, the women of our society enter purposefully into our armed forces and will kill, if necessary, to protect our country from the oppression and intrusion of other leaders.

In addition, one can see in her story the foreshadowing of man's sin being nailed to the cross. Sisera very well represents the contamination of sin in the land and the extreme measure that it would take to put it out. Jael nailed him in the temple of his head, representing in the natural sense, how to kill and prevent the venomous strike of a serpent. Our sins were nailed to the Cross through the shedding of Jesus Christ's blood, our Savior Who bore our sins.

> "For he (God) hath made him to be sin for us, who knew no sin; that we might be made the righteousness of God in him." 2 Corinthians 5:21

God allowed Christ to be identified with us as sinners and would not allow our sins that He bore to go unpunished.

Therefore, He (Jesus) was nailed to the Cross (Isa. 53:12; Ro. 8:32). What Jael did by killing Sisera was appropriate warfare at that time. God used her to fulfill prophecy and recorded it as an honor to her character in the Word of God. The Prophetess Deborah sung a victory song unto God, which included the praise of Jael as follows:

> (v24) Blessed above women shall Jael the wife of Heber the Kenite be, blessed shall she be above women in the tent. (v25) He asked water, and she gave him milk; she brought forth butter in a lordly dish. (v26) She put her hand to the nail, and her right hand to the workmen's hammer; and with the hammer she smote Sisera, she smote off his head, when she had pierced and stricken through his temples. (v27) At her feet he bowed, he fell, he lay down: at her feet he bowed, he fell: where he bowed, there he fell down dead. Judges 5:24-27

How does Jael's portrait encourage the virtuous woman in us?

I am not condoning a life being taken away by anyone, for any reason. However, I believe God wants women who have murdered someone in self-defense, fighting to save a country, or because they have felt trapped in a situation with no way out to be encouraged. These women may be outside of a physical prison, but they are yet unable to forgive themselves. Even if the murder was intentional, salvation, deliverance, and healing is available through repentance and the blood of Jesus Christ. Most often, these types of brutal acts occur while we are still sinners. Also, they may be due to the lack of spiritual understanding of our ability to overcome the enemy that seeks to destroy us. Some may remain sinners because they will not receive the gift of God (salvation) which is through Jesus Christ. They parade as if they have no conscience, but they are filled with deeply buried guilt.

I almost committed murder myself when my first husband was physically abusing me. Yes, even though I was a Christian, after this particular fight, I was faced with an ultimatum that seemed like there was no other alternative but to take the gun in my hands. After a huge fight that began at my parents' house, my husband and I returned home. He threatened to return to my parents' house with his shotgun and kill them while they were asleep. In my heart, I never considered he would fail to carry out his threat. After all, he had been shooting his gun for hours and we had fought all night. It was about 5:30 a.m. when he laid the pump shotgun down and started towards the bedroom to clean himself up and go as he said, "shoot up" my parents house while they slept. He entered the bedroom to change clothes, never knowing his life was being threatened.

With the panic of his threatening words echoing in my mind and spirit, I picked up the gun. I thought, If he had killed me it would have been better, but I could not let him kill my parents. As I picked up the gun, I prayed "Lord, if he comes out of the room dressed to go, I'm going to kill him. So, Lord "Please..." don't let him come out dressed. And "Please..." let something happen to this gun." I could see him coming down the hall before he could see me. He was not dressed and by faith, I laid the gun down and moved away from it. At that point, I saw the hand of God move and he began to reveal scriptural truths to me about spiritual warfare.

"For we wrestle not against flesh and blood, but against principalities, against powers, against the rulers of the darkness of this world, against spiritual wickedness in high places." Ephesians 6:12

My husband walked directly to the gun, picked it up and went to cock it again to shoot it. That is when God intervened, "THE WHOLE PUMP PART OF THE GUN FELL OFF". Praise God! The phone then rang. It was his mother. As he talked with her, I was amazed at the mild humble tone and mannerism he used while speaking to her. If I had not experienced the torment of that night and was the person on the other end of that phone, I would have believed too that all was well. He went into a rage as soon as he hung up the phone. I didn't know anything about spiritual warfare but God's peace came over me. It was as if, I was surrounded by His protection. Then I saw a demon. It came out of my husband and stood between my husband and me. It was as if, I was looking at two different people. When the demon spirit saw that I did not fear it, it went back into him and my husband, picked up my Bible, threw it at me and told me to "GET OUT!" Talking about an eye opener, I could really see the spiritual reality of what was happening.

My spiritual eyes were opened that morning. I was not fighting against flesh and blood. Ephesians 6:12 really came to life to me. I realized that if I had killed my husband that morning, I would not have killed the problem. That demonic spirit would have accomplished its purpose of taking my husband's life and destroying me in the process. The same demonic spirit would have left him and entered into another person's life with the same purpose to destroy that individual. This marriage ended. Going forward, I never again could look at another human being as the cause of a problem.

If you, for some reason, have taken a life under circumstances such as these examples presented, be assured the Lord still loves you and wants to do great things in your life. Furthermore, it doesn't matter if you committed the act while you were a sinner or a Christian and thought you were doing the right thing. God still can use you. Consider the Apostle Paul.

The Apostle Paul knew this truth very well. Prior to Paul's name being changed, his name was Saul. As Saul, he was deceived into thinking he was doing the right thing as he aggressively sought to kill Christians. In search of more Christians to kill, he met on his journey Jesus Christ, who changed his life forever (Acts 9:1-28). He was converted to Christianity. Remembering his life prior to becoming the Apostle Paul, he experienced plagues of struggles and condemnation. Instead of buckling underneath the stain of sin, he accepted the true mercies and grace of God for his life. As a result he became one of the greatest inspired authors of the Bible, writing over one third of the New Testament. Today billions of sinners are converted to Christianity because of his testimony. They are encouraged daily and strengthened through the gift of God that operated through him. Paul's personal testimony and his encounter with Jesus supplied us with spiritual insight and truth about the saving grace of God through Jesus Christ. The following few scriptures from his writings are most encouraging to me personally. They are able to guide the most hardened sinners into an abundant and divine life in Christ Jesus:

> "There is therefore now no condemnation to them which are in Christ Jesus, who walk not after the flesh, but after the Spirit." Romans 8:1

Once we believe and confess Christ, we can't help but to walk (seek) after the Spirit of God.

> (v27) And he that searcheth the hearts knoweth what is the mind of the Spirit, because he maketh intercession for the saints according to the will of God. (v28) And we know that all things work together for good to them that love God, to them who are the called according to his purpose. Romans 8:27-28

God has a purpose for all of us regardless of what we have done. Again, look at the life of the Apostle Paul.

What shall we then say to these things? If God be for us, who can be against us? Romans 8:31

Others may not forgive you but forgive them and forgive yourself. The Word of God says that when Judas came to betray Jesus, the Lord called him "**friend**" (Matt. 26:47-50). This was not a sarcastic remark from Jesus. Jesus loved Judas and was dying for his sins also. When Judas realized what he had done, Judas wanted to undo his betrayal of the Lord. He could not see living after this, although he could have. But instead, he went out and hung himself (Matt. 27:2-5). Judas was truly sorry for what he did by betraying Jesus but he could not forgive himself.

> (v35) Who shall separate us from the love of Christ? shall tribulation, or distress, or persecution, or famine, or nakedness, or peril, or sword? (v36) As it is written, FOR THY SAKE WE ARE KILLED ALL THE DAY LONG; WE ARE ACCOUNTED AS SHEEP FOR THE SLAUGHTER. (v37) Nay, in all these things we are more than conquerors

through him that loved us. (v38) For I am persuaded, that neither death, nor life, nor angels, nor principalities, nor powers, nor things present, nor things to come, (v39) Nor height, nor depth, nor any other creature, shall be able to separate us from the love of God, which is in Christ Jesus our Lord. Romans 8:35-39

The Lord will take on every one of our cares if we allow him to. Our burdens are His. Consider this resolution of the Apostle Paul,

(v10) That I may know him, and the power of his resurrection, and the fellowship of his sufferings, being made conformable unto his death; (v11) If by any means I might attain unto the resurrection of the dead. (v12) Not as though I had already attained, either were already perfect: but I follow after, if that I may apprehend that for which also I am apprehended of Christ Jesus. (v13) Brethren, I count not myself to have apprehended: but this one thing I do, forgetting those things which are behind, and reaching forth unto those things which are before, (v14) I press toward the mark for the prize of the high calling of God in Christ Jesus.   Philippians 3:10-14

We all can get to know God as our personal Savior, who saves us, changes us, uses us, loves us, cares for us, and helps us because that is the power of His resurrection. We too can resolve to forget those things that are behind us, with the intent of becoming all that God had in mind before we were conceived within our mother's womb.

PORTRAIT FIVE

"A Woman Who Knew She Was Unattractive and Hated"

LEAH

Genesis 29:26-30:21; 49:31

Who was Leah?

(v16) And Laban had two daughters: the name of the elder was Leah, and the name of the younger was Rachel. (v17) Leah was tender eyed; but Rachel was beautiful and well favored. Genesis 29:16-17

Leah is introduced to us in the Word of God as the first born of Laban's two daughters. In her life's story, God inspired the writer to place notable emphasis on both her and her sister's physical countenance. Leah is paraded as "tender-eyed". Some writers believe that her vision was probably dimming and that she could barely see. However, dimming eyes might not necessarily cause one to be unattractive. We could perhaps consider Leah to have been crossed-eyed, as well as, near sighted. This would certainly lend an excuse to her being less favorable to look upon. Laban said it was her age and their custom to marry the eldest first. Whether it was her less favorable countenance or her age, her

89

father, Laban, resorted to a deceitful decision to marry her off to a rising and promising descendent of Father Abraham and Isaac, whose name was Jacob. God later named Jacob, Israel because his twelve sons would establish the nation of Israel and implement the progressive covenant of restoration between God and man.

Thereby, Leah became the first wife of Jacob and gave birth to six of those twelve sons and a daughter.

What was Leah's wedding preparation and marriage consummation like?

(v20) And Jacob served seven years for Rachel; and they seemed unto him but a few days, for the love he had to her. (v21) And Jacob said unto Laban, Give me my wife, for my days are fulfilled, that I may go in unto her. (v22) And Laban gathered together all the men of the place, and made a feast. (v23) And it came to pass in the evening, that he took Leah his daughter, and brought her to him; and he went in unto her. (v24) And Laban gave unto his daughter Leah Zilpah his maid for an handmaid. (v25) And it came to pass, that in the morning, behold it was Leah: and he said to Laban, What is this thou hast done unto me? did not I serve with thee for Rachel? wherefore then hast thou beguiled me? (v26) And Laban said, It must not be so done in our country, to give the younger before the firstborn. (v27) fulfill her week, and we will give thee this also for the service which thou shalt serve with me yet seven other years. Genesis 29:20-27

The Word of God does not give us a great deal of details of how this wedding was planned. For seven years Jacob labored for the hand in marriage to Leah's sister Rachel, who he greatly loved. Did both Rachel and Leah know during this whole seven years period that their father was going to pull a fast one on Jacob by switching them on the wedding day? We don't know. We do know that this wedding was the only one of its kind recorded within the Word of God. We don't see the customary traditions of the two week marriage celebration taking place (Judges 14:12). Nor do we see an espousal period for Leah with Jacob (Matt. 1:18). The probability is high that there was no getting to know her future husband except from a distance. Did her sister Rachel enjoy the love sporting, teasing, and fellowship of Jacob during the seven years he thought he was going to marry her? There was no agreement of consent to properly marry Leah and Jacob. The agreement was for Rachel (Gen. 29:20). Did Rachel openly enjoy her sister's wedding celebration as if it were her own? We don't know. But, we do know that Laban threw a party where only the men attended that day. We can infer that Jacob got pretty stoned. He was so stoned that when Leah was brought in, he did not bother to remove her veil or to recognize who she was. Perhaps it was even too dark to tell. There on her wedding night, in consummation to and with her husband, she enjoyed perhaps her first and last passionate and blissful intimate encounter with her husband as "Rachel" and not herself, Leah. Yes... Jacob rendered to her his reasonable service as her husband, but never again would she enjoy such ravishing intimacy with her husband.

What were some of Leah's marital struggles?

It appears that Leah's married life imposed a great deal of torment to her heart. The first struggle we notice is that on her wedding night she pretended to be her sister Rachel. Once Jacob sobered and turned over to his new bride, he found her to be Leah. We can only imagine the shock, the offense, the violation, and betrayal Jacob must have felt to see that he had engaged in passionate intimacy and was now married to a woman that he found to be in total contempt to his desire. We have an account of how he responded to Laban (V25), but what was his immediate response to Leah? Realistically, he did not politely say, "Excuse me a moment while I go have a word with your father." No! Surely his reaction towards her was very honest and dramatic. She had to have experienced the eruption of his contempt for what had been done. More than likely Jacob did not calm down the same day and return to his bride for a blissful honeymoon. It probably took him awhile to come to terms with this deceitful betrayal. Thereby, Leah's years of heartaches had just begun.

For the next seven years, Leah struggled to build a meaningful relationship with her husband. Although she did not have to share her husband's physical commitment in the bedroom with her sister for the first seven years, she was in desperate competition with her sister to win over his love. Even as she looked upon their sporting and teasing each other in the field, and perhaps the laughter that took place between Rachel and her husband, Leah would not dare speak against his love for her. She knew that if she did speak to him of his love for Rachel, for any reason or with any displeasure in her voice, it would drive his heart further away from her. Leah's actions speaks clearly to us that she offered herself simply as a comforter to Jacob. She never expected his love, though she longingly and desperately desired it. She showered him with unconditional love. For a while Leah's love may have pacified him, but the Word says that God saw that she was "hated."

(v30) And he [Jacob] went in also unto Rachel, and he loved also Rachel more than Leah, and served with him yet seven other years. (v31) and When the Lord saw that Leah was hated, he opened her womb: but Rachel was barren.   Gen. 29:30-31

The word "hated" in this scripture means to hate an individual and to treat an individual as an enemy in the Hebrew language. Once the marriage of Jacob and Rachel was consummated, they both despised the very existence of Leah's presence between them. More so by Rachel. It is indicated that there came a time that Jacob withheld from his husbandry services to Leah because of his intimacy with Rachel. Rachel constantly contended with Leah to bare Jacob children. The only time Jacob went in unto Leah was when a bargain took place between she and Rachel.

And Rachel said, with great wrestling's have I wrestled with my sister, and I have prevailed: and she called his name Naphtali. Genesis 30:8

This left Leah in the position of bargaining with her sister to hire the service of her husband in the bedroom.

(v14) And Reuben went in the days of wheat harvest, and found mandrakes in the field, and brought them unto his mother Leah. Then Rachel said to Leah, Give me, I pray thee, of thy son's mandrakes. (v15) And she said unto her, Is it a small matter that thou hast taken my husband? and wouldest thou take away my son's mandrakes also? And Rachel said, Therefore he shall lie with thee to night for thy son's mandrakes. (v16) And Jacob came out of the field in the evening, and Leah went out to meet him, and said, Thou must come in unto me; for surely I have

93

hired thee with my son's mandrakes. And he lay with her that night. (V17) And God hearkened unto Leah, and she conceived, and bare Jacob the fifth son. (v18) And Leah said, God hath given me my hire, because I have given my maiden to my husband: and she called his name Issachar. Genesis 30:14-18

Certainly, Leah was the champion of child bearing with Jacob's seed to carry on his name between her and her sister. This still did not win over Jacob's love for her. No matter how sexy she tried to appear, no matter how creative in the bedroom she became, no matter how many children she gave him, Jacob was not in love with Leah. He was in love with Rachel. When Jacob felt his life to be threatened by the prospect of his brother Esau's revenge, he sent Leah and her children after the concubines to face the potential dangers first. This would allow an opportunity for Rachel and him to escape in the event they had faced his brother's wrath (Gen. 32- 33:2). In like manner, many women have had children in hopes of gaining love from a man. We can learn from Leah's experience that children do not stimulate and nurture love between a man and a woman. Nor does it make the man more responsive to the woman's needs.

Why and how did God encourage Leah through her struggles?

(v32) And Leah conceived, and bare a son, and she called his name Reuben: for she said, Surely the Lord hath looked upon my affliction; now therefore my husband will love me. (v33) And she conceived again, and bare a son; and said, Because the Lord hath heard that I was hated, he hath therefore given me this son also: and she called his name Simeon. (v34) And she conceived again, and bare a son; and said,

94

Now this time will my husband be joined unto me, because I have born him three sons: therefore was his name called Levi. (v35) And she conceived again, and bare a son: and she said, Now will I praise the Lord: therefore she called his name Judah; and left bearing. Genesis 29:32-35

(v17) And God hearkened unto Leah, and she conceived, and bare Jacob the fifth son. (v18) And Leah said, God hath given me my hire, because I have given my maiden to my husband: and she called his name Issachar. (v19) And Leah conceived again, and bare Jacob the sixth son. (v20) And Leah said, God hath endued me with a good dowry; now will my husband dwell with me, because I have born him six sons: and she called his name Zebulun. (v21) And afterwards she bare a daughter, and called her name Dinah. Genesis 30:17-21

God gave Leah a purpose to live outside of pleasing Jacob. Leah appeared to be a praying woman who embraced her husband's God, unlike her sister who stole her father's gods to worship (Gen. 31:34). She talked to God constantly about her marriage and her sufferings within the triune circle.

Constantly, Leah cried out for the love of her husband. Each time she conceived, she offered praise to God and declared her unfailing desire to gain her husband's love. Though Jacob loved his children and cared for Leah, his heart was fixed towards his love for Rachel. The children did not draw his heart towards Leah. However, Leah's children brought joy and added purpose to her life whereas before none had existed. Even Leah's maid gave birth to two sons that were credited unto Leah's tribes (Gen. 30:9-12). There in her wilderness of sufferings, she gladly cared for and nurtured her six plus two sons who grew to bring forth eight of the twelve perpetual kingdoms of Israel.

In similar situations to that of Leah's, there are many married women who oftentimes experience extreme loneliness and isolation being married to an unfaithful husband. The husband may be formally committed for decades to the marriage union but not to the married partner. Leah's life is also a champion of marital commitment and inspires our unconditional love that will preserve the family union.

What was the final crown of God's reward to Leah's faithfulness to Him?

Leah had no choices within her marriage except to choose to do Jacob good and that gift she exercised well. God knew of all Leah's bitter trials, but would not remove them. Instead, he gave her courage, grace, patience, peace, and strength to endure unto a victorious end. He bestowed the honors of the first and God chosen wife upon her. Not only was her quiver filled with the nations of God more so than her sister, she out lived her sister. In fact, Rachel died in bitter childbirth and was buried by the way of a journey before reaching Bethlehem (Gen. 35:16- 20).

I believe that God honored Jacob's love for Rachel because she was his choice of love. However, God honored Leah because of her extraordinary devotion and ability to bestow unconditional love upon her husband and her wholehearted reverence of God.

She demonstrates God's Agape love well throughout her trials. Leah lived a well-seasoned life and because of her faith, she was buried in honor with the legendary hall of faith members, Abraham, Sarah, Isaac, and Rebekah (Gen. 49:31). These are the eternal glories that will never pass away throughout "all" generation. One could say that Leah was the Alpha (beginning) and Omega (ending) of her marriage union. Seeing that Rachel died giving birth to her second child, it is likely that Leah even trained up Rachel's children. God's favor upon her life caused her to rear the men who would form the twelve tribes of Israel.

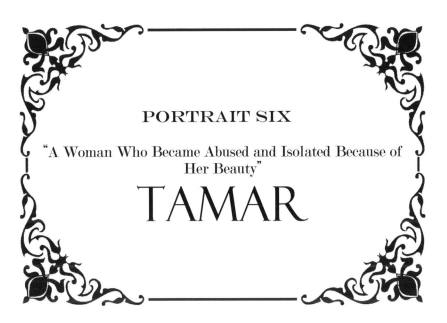

PORTRAIT SIX

"A Woman Who Became Abused and Isolated Because of Her Beauty"

TAMAR

II Samuel 13; I Chronicles 3:9

Who was Tamar?

"And it came to pass after this, that Absalom the son of David had a fair sister, whose name was Tamar..." II Samuel 13:1a

"These were all the sons of David, beside the sons of the concubines, and Tamar their sister." I Chronicles 3:9

This particular Tamar was a real life "beautiful princess". She was born to the marriage union of King David and Queen Maachah. Tamar grew up in a palace kingdom. Her father had many wives and concubines. Although she had the probability of having many stepbrothers and stepsisters, she was the only daughter of King David's to be mentioned in the scriptures. She was first mentioned in the scriptures as Absalom's "fair sister". She had, however, only one full brother, Absalom and he loved her very much.

What were Tamar's qualities?

(v8) So Tamar went to her brother Amnon's house; and he was laid down. And she took flour, and kneaded it, and made cakes in his sight, and did bake the cakes. (v9) And she took a pan, and poured them out before him...

(v18) And she had a garment of diverse colours upon her: for with such robes were the king's daughters that were virgins apparelled... II Samuel 13:8-9, 18

Tamar was not only beautiful, but she was not spoiled as one would suppose a princess would be. She dressed like a promising and flowering princess indicated by her "garment of many colors". Everyone around her knew of her chaste and virtuous demeanor and respected her. Though she dressed royally, another quality she possessed was, Tamar could "burn in the kitchen". Its evident in the scriptures that Tamar took great pride in learning how to grow into a mature woman with the hopes of someday marrying and caring for her own family. She demonstrated her ability well by taking the flour, kneading it and baking cakes. As the scriptures narrates her cooking abilities, one can imagine the aroma that filled Amnon's chamber that day.

In addition, Tamar was wise and courageous in her speech. When Amnon, her stepbrother approached her with his indecent proposal, Tamar tried to reason with him without offending him. She appealed, with her words, to his consciousness regarding what the consequences would be if such an indecent act was to occur between them out of wedlock. Thus, she begged him to do the right thing and that was to ask her father properly for her hand in marriage.

(v11) And when she had brought them unto him to eat, he took hold of her, and said unto her, Come lie with me, my sister. (12) And she answered him, Nay, my brother, do not force me; for no such thing ought to be done in Israel: do not thou this folly. (v13) And I, whither shall I cause my shame to go? and as for thee, thou shalt be as one of the fools in Israel. Now therefore, I pray thee, speak unto the king; for he will not withhold me from thee. II Samuel 13:11-13

What indecency and Why did Amnon seek out against Tamar?

(v1) And it came to pass after this, that Absalom the son of David had a fair sister, whose name was Tamar; and Amnon the son of David loved her. (v2) And Amnon was so vexed, that he fell sick for his sister Tamar; for she was a virgin; and Amnon thought it hard for him to do any thing to her. (v3) But Amnon had a friend, whose name was Jonadab, the sons of Shimeah David's brother: and Jonadab was a very subtle man. (v4) And he said unto him, Why art thou, being the king's sons, lean from day to day? wilt thou not tell me? And Amnon said unto him, I love Tamar, my brother Absalom's sister. (v5) And Jonadab said unto him, Lay thee down on thy bed, and make thyself sick: and when thy father cometh to see thee, say unto him, I pray thee, let my sister Tamar come, and give me meat, and dress the meat in my sight, that I may see it, and eat it at her hand. (v6) So Amnon lay down, and made himself sick: and when the king was come to see him, Amnon said unto the king, I pray thee, let Tamar my sister come, and make me a couple of cakes in my sight, that I may eat at her hand. (v7) Then David sent home to

101

Tamar, saying, Go now to thy brother Amnon's house,
and dress him meat.   II Samuel 13:1-7

The word "fair" in the scriptures means very pleasant to look upon or very beautiful. Tamar's physical beauty was coupled with her inner beauty. These two characteristics combined are quite noticeable to men and are most often preyed upon by them.

The story of Tamar brings home the truth for many women across the land. The violation of rape against Tamar because of her physical appearance was awful enough but the person who raped her made it more gruesome. The enemy used two of her family members to implement his plan of destruction against her life.

Amnon fell lustfully sick in love with his stepsister Tamar. He had contemplated over and over in his mind as to how he could lay with her without consideration to asking the king for her hand in marriage. At some point, he must have considered the resulting consequences if he forced Tamar to lay with him. The scriptures say in verse 2, **Amnon thought it hard for him to do anything to her.** He knew by taking her virginity away, he would do irreversible damage to her life, as well as, exile her to dishonor. This same dishonor is still common today. Amnon knew that he would be taking the most precious gift that Tamar would have to offer a husband and that was, "herself". Nevertheless, Amnon was the king's son and was accustomed to having his way with women. He could pick and choose from among all the beautiful women in the land and make them his concubines (informal wives) as he pleased. Instead, he chose to set his desire upon his stepsister Tamar. His lusts lead to his obsession of her.

Amnon became tormented in his spirit and was driven into action by his lust for Tamar. All he needed was a plan to get her alone. When his cousin Jonadab, who was also his most trusted friend, came to see him, Amnon confided in him. Together, the two men conspired, mapped out, and implemented a very detailed plan for Amnon to fulfill his desire (verses 5-7). Unaware of this treacherous plan, Tamar became a snared victim of rape:

> "Howbeit he would not hearken unto her voice: but, being stronger than she, forced her, and lay with her."
> II Samuel 13:14

This is how the enemy seeks to destroy our lives. He forms weapons against us and seeks opportunities to successfully carry them out.

What happened to Tamar after Amnon raped her?

> (v15) Then Amnon hated her exceedingly; so that the hatred wherewith he hated her was greater than the love wherewith he had loved her. And Amnon said unto her, Arise, be gone. (v16) And she said unto him, There is no cause: this evil in sending me away is greater than the other that thou didst unto me. But he would not hearken unto her. (v17) Then he called his servant that ministered unto him, and said, Put now this woman out from me, and bolt the door after her. (v18) And she had a garment of divers colors upon her: for with such robes were the king's daughters that were virgins apparelled. Then his servant brought her out, and bolted the door after her. II Samuel 13:15-18

There is an agony of the soul that exists in life that surpasses man's ability to explain it. Oftentimes, when this type of pain is encountered, it leaves one with no recourse but to find refuge in their own moans and groans. This is the type of pain that

Tamar encountered both physically and mentally through Amnon's premeditated scheme to rape her. After forcefully taking Tamar, Amnon's passionate and lustful desire, which he once called love, turned immediately to hostile contempt **"hate"** of her being in his presence. He had taken what was most precious to her and then without hesitation, he thrust her away, banishing her from before him permanently.

Once the physical violation was over, Tamar must have been flooded with thoughts of "what's going to happen to me next?" If for one moment she had considered that this was an act of his overwhelming love for her and that afterwards he would consider doing the right thing "marry her to himself", that thought was quickly dispelled. The truth was cruel and it scorned and tormented her more deeply when she heard his words **"arise, be gone"**. If the wrong could have been righted, Amnon never gave it a chance. He had his servant literally throw her out while she was pleading with him not to totally dishonor her. The servant locked the door to prevent her reentrance. Tamar's whole world was torn apart and she would never be the same again.

Tamar lived the rest of her life in desolation. Why?

(v19) And Tamar put ashes on her head, and rent her garment of divers colours that was on her, and laid her hand on her head, and went on crying. (v20) And Absalom her brother said unto her, Hath Amnon thy brother been with thee? but hold now thy peace, my sister: he is thy brother; regard not this thing. So Tamar remained desolate in her brother Absalom's house. (v21) But when king David heard of all these things, he was very wroth.   II Samuel 13:19-21

Unlike many women, Tamar knew the significance of her virginity before loosing it. All around the world, even in the Christian Church, a sexual promiscuous lifestyle has been passed on from generation to generation. This results primarily from the lack of knowledge of how sacred intimate relations should be. It is key to communicate that knowledge in a loving and encouraging way and to live its sentiments by example before our children. It is failure not to reiterate the appropriateness of when intimate relationships are suppose to occur. Another reason that promiscuous behaviors exist among women is failure to maintain the standard of consecration. At age thirteen, when the first rape took place in my life, I knew that a violation had taken place, but I had no idea of the importance of my virginity. I had not been taught such significance. My mother did not know how to communicate such intimate matters to me. So, I took advice from peers who barely knew more than I did and consequently, I continued to live a promiscuous lifestyle. This was not the case in Tamar's situation.

Tamar was taught extensively the significance of her virginity and the significance of not loosing it before marriage. It was customary that all the people, this included boys and girls, were taught the laws of God governing sexual conduct. God addressed the potential of every scenario of relationship and sexual conduct and provided laws to follow in the event that they occurred. Those laws included the violation of rape:

> (v28) If a man find a damsel that is a virgin, which is not betrothed, and lay hold on her, and lie with her, and they be found; (v29) Then the man that lay with her shall give unto the damsel's father fifty shekels of silver, and she shall be his wife; because he hath humbled her, he may not put her away all his days. Deut. 22:28-29

Although this was rape against Tamar, she was (according to the law) now his concubine, his inferior wife. This is why Tamar said, **There is no cause; this evil in sending me away is greater than the other that thou didst unto me (v16).** Tamar lost all of her joy and hope that day of ever having a fruitful life. She gave over the rest of her life to mourning, sorrow of soul and isolation. Utterly distorted and cast down within her spirit, Tamar covered her hair with the filth of ashes and ripped off her honorable robe of purity. Then the Word says, and **she went on crying**. Tamar relived that day, every day, for as long as she lived. Every single day, she grieved the loss of her bedroom innocence that was so violently taken away from her and no one came to her rescue.

Was living in desolation a virtuous act by Tamar?

There was also a law governing against a man who wrongfully hate's and put away his wife after the consummation of their wedding night:

> (v13) If any man take a wife, and go in unto her, and hate her, (v14) And give occasions of speech against her, and bring up an evil name upon her, and say, I took this woman, and when I came to her, I found her not a maid: (v15) Then shall the father of the damsel, and her mother, take and bring forth the tokens of the damsel's virginity unto the elders of the city in the gate: (v16) And the damsel's father shall say unto the elders, I gave my daughter unto this man to wife, and he hateth her; (v17) And, lo, he hath given occasions of speech against her, saying, I found not thy daughter a maid; and yet these are the tokens of my daughter's virginity. And they shall spread the cloth before the elders of the city. (v18) And the elders of that city shall take that man and chastise

him; (v19) And they shall amerce him in a hundred shekels of silver, and give them unto the father of the damsel, because he hath brought up an evil name upon a virgin of Israel: and she shall be his wife; he may not put her away all his days. Deuteronomy 22:13-19

In Tamar's culture, this was a very virtuous and noble act for Tamar to remain celibate in her brother's house. Tamar understood the blood covenant that took place between a husband and wife on the night of the marriage consummation. She knew all the laws including the one where a man might seek to put away his wife or dishonor her reputation by accusing her of infidelity before their consummation. Tamar was forced to submit to the humiliation of being humbled, but refused to compromise the standard of purity in her heart.

There was only one possible witness of what had taken place between Amnon and Tamar and that was the servant that put her out and locked the door behind her at Amnon's request. All of the evidence that would have proven her virtue was destroyed and of course, Amnon would not own up to violating her. Once her full brother, Absalom, perceived the truth, he appeared to protect the reputation of his half-brother. Instead of charging Amnon with doing the right thing, he responded by telling his sister to keep silent and to overlook it as if it had not happened. In like manner, when her father, King David heard about what happened to his daughter, he was very angry but did nothing about it. He disregarded the impact that the rape had on Tamar. All three men ignored God's laws and discounted the virtue of Tamar as insignificant. The two most important men in her life (her father and her brother) were willing to refrain from properly imposing vindication on her behalf against Amnon. This very fact re-enforced Tamar's hopelessness that there was nowhere to turn for comfort and no way to make things right again. Thus, maintaining her own innocence and virtue, she resolved not to submit to a profaned lifestyle.

Was Tamar ever vindicated?

(v22) And Absalom spake unto his brother Amnon neither good or bad: for Absalom hated Amnon, because he had forced his sister Tamar.

(v27) Now Absalom pressed him (King David), that he let Amnon and all the king's sons go with him. (v28) Now Absalom had commanded his servants, saying, Mark ye now when Amnon's heart is merry with wine, and when I say unto you, Smite Amnon; then kill him, fear not: have not I commanded you? be courageous, and be valiant. (v29) And the servants of Absalom did unto Amnon as Absalom had commanded. Then all the king's sons arose, and every man gat him up upon his mule, and fled.

(v32) And Jonadab, the son of Shimeah David's brother, answered and said, Let not my lord suppose that they have slain all the young men the king's sons; for Amnon only is dead: for by the appointment of Absalom this hath been determined from the day that he forced his sister Tamar. II Samuel 13:22, 27-29, 32

Woe unto the man whom offenses come through against the innocent! Murder is not the answer today because vengeance belongs to our God (Gen. 4:15). He is **a very present help in the time of trouble** by the power of the Holy Ghost working in our lives. However, the fate of judgment does come to our lives unless true repentance takes place and we turn to do the right thing. **Be not**

deceived; God is not mocked: for whatsoever a man soweth, that shall he also reap (Gal. 6:7). Amnon did not escape this principle of God's integrity towards His Word. Absalom watched his sister's soul cry out daily for two years. To him, it was as though a baby had been wounded and crippled for life, all because a lustful thief senselessly took what he could have had lawfully. Her tormenting cries of innocence drove him to vindicate her. Just as Amnon had carefully devised a plan to take Tamar's virginity, Absalom bridled his anger for two years and brooded over a premeditated plan to kill him and did. Thus, even King David came to peace with his son's (Amnon) death and forgave Absalom for killing him.

And the soul of King David longed to go forth unto Absalom: for he was comforted concerning Amnon, seeing he was dead. II Sam. 13:39

How does Tamar's virtuous image encourage us?

Amnon was the king's son and Tamar's was the king's daughter. Their father had a desire that they both would live and therefore, would not impose judgment upon Amnon at the time he violated his sister. However, there came a time that vindication was executed on the behalf of Tamar and her father was at peace with the death of his son, Amnon. This was because Amnon had failed to repent of his wickedness and it continued to bring about destruction within the family.

As brothers and sisters in Christ Jesus, oftentimes, we violate each other in the area of intimate relationships and refuse to do the right thing. We hurt each other and have no idea what results from the poisoning tares we sow into each other's lives. Notwithstanding, when we know we have hurt each other and we refuse the responsibility of trying to make it right. God is long suffering to all men, even when we trespass against each other, in hopes that all will repent and be saved (II Pet. 3:9). But, there will come a day that judgment will come and God will execute judgment against any man or woman who has committed such violating acts against His daughters or His sons. Even in such cases of promiscuous living where men and women are refusing the covenant of marriage:

> "Marriage is honorable in all, and the bed undefiled: but whoremongers and adulterers God will judge."
> Hebrews 13:4

Meanwhile, we must do like Tamar and crucify the flesh. Tamar was a king's daughter and nothing could make her doubt or compromise the standard that she had been so diligently taught regarding a virtuous woman and an intimate relationship. She would not allow the trespasses or rejection of her brother cause her to lose her royal dignity. Tamar became married to righteousness and remained true to the standard of holy living. We too must recognize that God is the only one that is able to pick us up after rejection and give us a new life. As we rely on him to heal us, sustain us, and bless us in our relationships, His mercies will put our broken lives back together and enable us to live abundant lives.

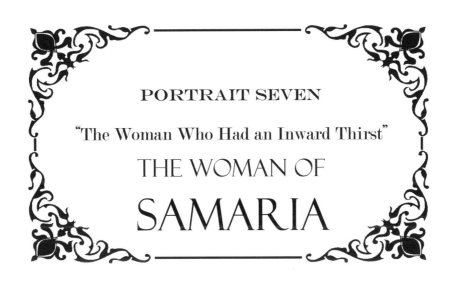

"The Woman Who Had an Inward Thirst"

THE WOMAN OF
SAMARIA

John 4:4-42

There are many perspectives from which we can look into the life of this woman from Samaria. For the purpose of this book, we will look into her more personal and intimate desires as a woman, her conversion and her virtuous contribution to the Kingdom of God.

Who was the woman of Samaria?

The details of her genealogy are not told to us. All we know about her family life is that she had five husbands and one in addition to them in which she was living with. Whether or not the other five husbands were yet living and had divorced her or if they were deceased is not known. It could have been that she lived as a concubine with her previous husbands and was sent away. We do not know. What we do know is that she faced many great trials in the area of relationships. Surprisingly in her sinful state of being, she had some knowledge of God's promise of a Messiah and expressed some hope in his coming.

"The woman saith unto him, I know that Messias cometh, which is called Christ: when he is come, he will tell us all things." John 4:25

There, at that well, she dared to express to Christ her belief in the coming Messiah and how He would clear up all of life's mysteries. This woman was not a woman who would readily talk of spiritual things. She knew she was sinful and therefore, moved with caution in speaking of such matters. But, there at the well with Christ, her inward thoughts, secrets, and thirst to live holy was being quenched by the Messiah, Himself.

Did the woman of Samaria possess an inward thirst?

The Bible says that God has dealt to every man the measure of faith (Rom. 12:3). Thank God! This one measure is the very thing that keeps us living despite the trials we go through. It is the one measure of faith that will produce a thirst within every living soul that the Master delights to show-up and quench with His eternal spring of living water. It is the seed that is designed by God to search for the light of "The Son" when the dark despair of sin grabs hold of our day and makes it seem like there is no tomorrow. Everyone at some point in their life will experience this thirst. But, will they receive the life sustaining water that gives increase to their faith?

There were days in my life, especially during my first marriage, that I just wanted to quit. The situation became unbearable. I was uneducated and I was hurting. My heart seemed to bleed nothing but sorrow. I just existed and it seemed as though I was loosing my mind. Of course, no one else knew what I was thinking. Somehow confidence leaped through my personality. But inside, I was falling apart. One particular morning while in a state of panic, I desired God to give me some answers that would heal my ever wounded and bleeding heart. I had what I call "a temper tantrum" with Him. I read about His goodness... I heard about His goodness... I talked about His goodness... I looked for His goodness... But after suffering so much, His goodness seemed to escape me. I took my Bible in hand and threw it against the wall and I yelled at God:

"You say that you are this awesome God and that you love everybody; and that you will meet all of our needs; heal our broken hearts, and etc... etc... etc... Well, I'm better than you are! If I knew someone was hurting and I had the power to do something about it, I would!"

Then I cried uncontrollably. All the time, my heart was hoping with the measure of faith that He had placed within me that He would hear the cry of my heart, heal my heart and give me a reason to keep going. As I sat down on the sofa, the television was on. The 700 Club was on with Pat Roberts and a woman co-host by name, Terry Meeuwsen. She began to prophesy, "There is a lady sitting at home on your couch. You cry day and night but, God is going to change those tears in to joyful tears." I knew she was talking to me. As she spoke, the Holy Spirit was speaking her words through my mouth. When no one else was around or knew my sorrows, the Lord heard my cry. I faced a few more years of trials within that marriage, but God showed up just for me that day. That day Jesus showed up on the television tube just to give me living water and that living water sustains me even until this day. He did the same thing for the Woman of Samaria as He showed up at the well.

(v4) And he must needs go through Samaria. (v5) Then cometh he to a city of Samaria, which is called Sychar, near to the parcel of ground that Jacob gave to his son Joseph. (v6) Now Jacob's well was there. Jesus therefore, being wearied with his journey, sat thus on the well: and it was about the sixth hour. (v7) There cometh a woman of Samaria to draw water: Jesus saith unto her, Give me to drink. (v8) (For his disciples were gone away unto the city to buy meat.) (v9) Then saith the woman of Samaria unto him, How is it that thou, being a Jew, askest drink of me, which am a woman of Samaria? for the Jews have no dealings with the Samaritans. (v10) Jesus answered and said unto her, If thou knewest the gift of God, and who it is that saith to thee, Give me to drink; thou wouldest have asked of him, and he would have given thee living water. John 4:4-10

It is believed by some that Jesus' destination to another place was the only cause of His passing through Samaria. Jesus disciples often misinterpreted His words and actions. When they tried to get Him to eat look at what happened:

(v31) In the mean while his disciples prayed him, saying, Master, eat. (v32) But he said unto them, I have meat to eat that ye know not of. (v33) Therefore said the disciples one to another, Hath any man brought him ought to eat? (v34) Jesus saith unto them, My meat is to do the will of him that sent me, and to finish his work. John 4:31-34

This woman did not just walk up to the well by chance and meet Jesus that day. Jesus was about his Father's business. He is "all knowing" and He is "a matter of fact" God. There are no idle words in Him. Jesus took this journey on purpose that day and stayed behind at the well alone on purpose because he had a gift for a woman whom desperately thirsted for the opportunity to get her life right with God. Jesus asked her for a drink. He knew that she appreciated the gift of Jacob's well and had reverenced God in her heart for the gifts of the forefathers of promise in the past. Jesus knew that her hope would identify Him with the fathers of divine promise and even as one greater than them all. He let her know that He had a gift to offer her and that it would quench her desire for all eternity. She then ask the questions:

> (v11) The woman saith unto him, Sir, thou hast nothing to draw with, and the well is deep: from whence then hast thou that living water? (v12) Art thou greater than our father Jacob, which gave us the well, and drank thereof himself, and his children, and his cattle?   John 4:11-12

This Woman of Samaria, though living in sin, was very confident in speaking of father Jacob. She called him "our father". It appears that she had pondered over the truth of God's covenant to mankind. Perhaps she heard of Jacob's trickery in stealing his brother's blessings and how that God still made him a covenant father of blessings (Gen. 27- 32). Pondering over the truth of how God brought others out of their sins and blessed them will encourage us in our discouragement. Whatever the truth was that sustained her hope, she was very confident in it and of what she knew about father Jacob. Seeing she had such great conviction in her confession of father Jacob, Jesus introduced her to a greater spiritual truth of how the thirst of the heart and soul could be extinguished.

> (v13) Jesus answered and said unto her, whosoever drinketh of this water shall thirst again: (v14) But whosoever drinketh of the water that I shall give him

shall never thirst; but the water that I shall give him shall be in him a well of water springing up into everlasting life.   John 4:13-14

She didn't fully understand what Jesus was talking about and that He had come in answer to her heart's cry. But, the truth of God's word, through Jesus, identified with the measure of faith that was within her. She knew He could do exactly what He said He could do. She asked Him to give her this water.

"The woman saith unto him, Sir, give me this water, that I thirst not, neither come hither to draw." John 4:15

She had not realized that He knew the thirst of her soul.

(v16) Jesus saith unto her, Go, call thy husband, and come hither (v17) The woman answered and said, I have no husband. Jesus said unto her, Thou hast well said, I have no husband: (v18) For thou hast had five husbands; and he whom thou now hast is not thy husband: in that saidst thou truly. John 4:16-18

Look at Jesus' response, **"Go, call thy husband, and come thither."** In answer to her request for living water, he addressed her relationships with men. Once promiscuous relationships are permitted into one's life, one may ask the question, "Can I ever be made whole, or get off this path of destruction?" In my single life, I have asked this very question. I have told God, "God I don't want to continue in this cycle of sin... I'm tired of changing partners... I want to live holy... I desire a husband who loves God and is God fearing. I want him to especially love me through a covenant, according to Your divine plan for holy matrimony." I can only image her praying within her heart some of the same sentiments I have expressed. Praying that the cycle would end and for courage to face tomorrow. Jesus let her know that God sees all by revealing that He knew her secret situation and was able to give her what she needed to live.

I can visualize the deliverance and healing that began to take place on the inside of this woman. Her spirit began to rejoice because she had met Jesus. This woman of Samaria then does an extraordinary thing. She humbled herself to acknowledge the presence of a prophet and asked questions of Him who had the real authority. She asked about worship. She wanted to know how to properly worship God.

> (v19) The woman saith unto him, Sir, I perceive that thou art a prophet. (v20) Our fathers worshipped in this mountain; and ye say, that in Jerusalem is the place where men ought to worship. (v21) Jesus saith unto her, Woman, believe me, the hour cometh, when ye shall neither in this mountain, nor yet at Jerusalem, worship the Father. (v22) Ye worship ye know not what: we know what we worship: for salvation is of the Jews. (v23) But the hour cometh, and now is, when the true worshippers shall worship the Father in spirit and in truth: for the Father seeketh such to worship him. (v24) God is a Spirit: and they that worship him must worship him in spirit and in truth. John 4:19-24

Does she learn how to worship in spirit and in truth?

> (v25) The woman saith unto him, I know that Messias cometh, which is called Christ: when he is come, he will tell us all things. (v26) Jesus saith unto her, I that speak unto thee am he. (v28) The woman then left her water pot, and went her way into the

city, and saith to the men, (v29) Come, see a man, which told me all things that ever I did: is not this the Christ? John 4:25-26; 28-29

Yes! She expected, received, and freely testified of the Christ presence at the well. The true spirit of worship gripped her soul until she was unable to contain herself. She left behind her water pot and bellowed praises throughout the town, **"Come see a man... Come see a man... Is not this the Christ?"** With her testimony, she compelled men to come, **"He told me all things that ever I did."** In truth she testified of her sin. She rejoiced in spirit and in truth that the Savior, Jesus the Christ, had come to give her life.

What was her virtuous contribution to the Kingdom of God?

There have been times in my life that God has bestowed such unconditional love upon me that it raised the standard in my love towards Him. It was during the time when I committed adultery, was constantly in fornication, and faced spiritual cowardliness towards my future. It was His gift of love that nurtured me to life and made me want to open up the heart of every hurting man, woman, boy, and girl and pour all that I knew about his sustaining power of love into them.

This Woman of Samaria did just that. She was on fire with the message of Jesus Christ and the whole town came to see what she was so excited about.

(v30) Then they went out to the city, and came unto him.

(v39) And many of the Samaritans of that city believed on him for the saying of the woman, which testified, He told me all that ever I did. (v40) So when the Samaritans were come unto him, they besought him that he would tarry with them: and he abode there two days. (v41) And many more believed because of his own word; (42) And said unto the woman, Now we believe, not because of thy saying: for we have heard him ourselves, and know that this is indeed the Christ, the Savior of the world. John 4:30, 39-42

The Woman of Samaria did not care that some folks of the town detested her very womanhood. She was not selfish with the Kingdom gift of the Savior. She did not go away receiving living water only to herself. No! She pries open the hearts of the town's people with her praise. Her voice echoed in the streets with resounding praises never heard before by anyone. Though some had no respect for her, they saw the immediate change in her, and heard her fervent testimony. This stirred them to at least go and see what had convinced her that the Messiah, the Christ, had come. She made a joyful noise that the humble could hear thereof and be glad (Ps. 34). Salvation had come! This woman possessed the honor of being the first evangelist of her town and for two days the people of that city could freely drink of the same living water through Jesus Christ.

Matt. 9:20-22 Luke 8:43-48; Mark 5:25-35

How did this nameless woman get recorded

in the Word of God?

What does it take to get into the Guinness World Book of Records? It is simple. Just do something no one else has done and make it work or achieve beating a standing record in whatever. Your name, the date, and category of accomplishment will be recorded for all to see. Eventually, someone will become interested enough in what has been accomplished and will come along and intentionally try to beat the existing record. It starts with a desire to achieve the same remarkable standard at a higher level. It is a choice... People set goals deliberately to go down in history like their forerunners! They know that the goal can be achieved because, someone has already accomplished it. They just want to do it better and usually they can because knowledge and resources increase with time that helps make the achievement greater.

In the Kingdom of God there is a Book of Life that records our achievements through faith (Rev. 20:12). It records whether or not we believe God at His Word and whether or not we act upon it to receive His blessings. These blessing supply us with what is needed to victoriously overcome the devil. The Bible is an earthly example of such recordings to give us the standard, the knowledge and resources to accomplish the same remarkable standard of our names being recorded in the Book of Life. This nameless woman became a high standard for faith healing to be accomplished in our live

> (v20) And, behold a woman, which was diseased with an issue of blood twelve years, came behind him, and touched the hem of his garment: (v21) For she said within herself, If I may but touch his garment, I shall be whole. (v22) But Jesus turned him about, and when he saw her, he said, Daughter, be of good comfort; thy faith hath made thee whole. And the woman was made whole from that hour. Matthew 9:20-22

What was her condition?

She was dying a slow death from a blood disorder within her body. This blood disorder caused her feminine cycle to hemorrhage for twelve long years. She could see death coming and there was nothing she could do about it. Perhaps she had even seen other women die from the same disorder. There was no cure available. Amazingly though, this woman looked death in the eye and said within herself, Somehow I am going to beat you! I am going to live! It is understood that she paid to become a study case for doctors to find a cure. They did not know how to treat this condition but at her request they would guess at cures until all of her money was spent. They failed in their attempts to find a cure, as well as, to slow down the process of her dying.

> (v25) And a certain woman, which had an issue of blood twelve years, (v26) And had suffered many things of many physicians, and had spent all that she had, and was nothing bettered, but rather grew worse. Mark 5:25-26

This illness caused her life activities to be confined to running back and forth from her house to the doctor's office. The rituals of the law in the land considered women to be unclean during the time of their feminine cycle and the women were forbidden to come out into the public, or to join in on any public activities. These restrictions included the temple, as well as, religious ceremonies (Gen. 31:35; Lev. 12:2- 7). This incurable disease seemed to possess the victory over this woman's struggle to live. No amount of money could purchase her healing. No human could help her. And what was worse, she was restricted from going to the temple. But, she never gave up hope! I believe God would not let her hope die within. Evidently, someone who loved her very much went back from one of Jesus' meetings and witnessed to her about Him. They told her of His message and of His healing power and she received the message of Christ gladly.

What did she do with the message that she heard about Jesus?

She became a newborn believer in Jesus Christ by the testimony of others.

> "When she had heard of Jesus, [she] came in the press behind, and touched his garment." Mark 5:27

123

From the very same moment that Jesus was passing by, she believed Jesus was able to perform miracles. Somehow after encountering numerous of disappointments from doctors and doing all she could do to be healed, she found the courage to believe that she could be blessed with healing from the Lord. She not only believed but she expected healing. The crowd around him overwhelmed Jesus. There was barely standing room for all the people who needed healing and came to hear His words. One way or another, she was going to get close enough to Jesus to be healed just by touching the very bottom of his garment.

This was the very least that she could do to exercise her faith and receive her healing. So she pressed... and pressed... She could have thought of herself as being insignificant or that it was impossible for her to get close enough to Jesus to receive her healing. However, there was not a doubt in her mind that healing was going to take place. She did not waste her energy by screaming and yelling trying to get Jesus' attention, but she quietly pressed her way to just be able to touch His clothing.

"For she said, If I may touch but his clothes, I shall be whole. "Mark 5:28

What happened when she touched His garment?

Her faith kept her pressing through the crowd until she reached her goal. She touched the hem of His garment.

This nameless woman set forth a faith breaking record in her generation. She received divine healing for all the world of Christians to see.

(v29) And straightway the fountain of her blood was dried up; and she felt in her body that she was healed of that plague. (v30) And Jesus, immediately knowing in himself that virtue had gone out of him, turned him about in the press, and said, Who touched me? (v31) And his disciples said unto him, Thou seest the multitude thronging thee, and sayest thou, Who touched me? (v32) And he looked round about to see her that had done this thing. (v33) But the woman fearing and trembling, knowing what was done in her, came and fell down before him, and told him all the truth. (v34) And he said unto her, Daughter, thy faith hath made thee whole; go in peace, and be whole of thy plague. Mark 5:29-34

There were so many people gathered around Jesus that she really thought herself too insignificant to gain his attention. Her thoughts were to just touch His clothing to receive healing and go away quietly.

But, her touch of faith could not go unnoticed. Out of all the people in the crowd that was gathered to receive something from Christ, pulling, tugging, grabbing at Him; she was the only one that received a miracle with no effort on Jesus' part. She received because of her faith. Faith the size of a mustard seed exercised will grant us our partitions before God (Matt. 17:20). This woman was a believer in the one and only God, Jehovah. She had now come into a new revelation of Jesus Christ that had come to save, heal, and set men free. Healing was hers for the asking. She commanded that the sickness in her body recognize the authority of her faith in Jesus Christ. The spirit of infirmity that trespassed with disease in her body had no choice but to dry up. Jesus could not ignore such astounding faith that drew virtue from Him. He called her forth and commended her faith. Today, we have her testimony of divine healing when the doctors cannot do us any good. We can expect healing!

Certainly, I have used her testimony to believe God for my healing through Jesus Christ. When we are in sin and lack knowledge of God's divine healing that is just waiting for us to receive; the devil and his demonic influences will trespass against us. Even when we are Christians, Satan will try to impose affliction upon us with all kinds of diseases. He counts on you and me will not believing in the healing benefits of the Cross. He has plagued our society with incurable disease such as AIDS, cancer, hepatitis and the list goes on. These diseases are presently incurable just as her blood disorder was then. But the same power that healed her is able to heal us.

One night while lying in bed, I heard the voice of a demon say, "I'm going to kill you!" Angry, I jumped out of bed and shouted back at him, "You don't have the power to kill me!" And, I laughed at the devil. A few months later I began to grow extremely tired in just performing simple, everyday task. To walk upstairs and downstairs at work became almost impossible. So, I made a doctor's appointment. After a few visits, I was diagnosed with hepatitis B, which there is no cure. The doctors ran a series of tests and tried to trace down how I contracted it. Was it during a dental visit? Was it from a blood transfusion I had received during surgery? Who knows? Then I remembered what the devil had spoken to me that day and this woman's story kept echoing in my spirit. I refused to continue to run to the doctor for something that the enemy had sown into my life. I knew this was something that man could do nothing about. The doctor asked me, "Do you want to live?"I asked her, "Is there a cure?" "No", she replied.

"Then I'll go to the Word of God." I said. Daily, I rebuked the enemy with God's Word with such like scriptures:

> (v2) Bless the Lord, O my soul, and forget not all his benefits: (v3) Who forgiveth all thine iniquities; who healeth all thy diseases. Psalms 103:2-3

"He sent his word, and healed them, and delivered them from their destructions." Psalms 107:20

"Behold, I give unto you power to tread on serpents and scorpions, and over all the power of the enemy: and nothing shall by any means hurt you." Luke 10:19

"Who hath delivered us from the power of darkness, and hath translated us into the kingdom of his dear Son." Colossians 1:13

> "But he was wounded for our transgressions; he was bruised for our iniquities: the chastisement of our peace was upon him; and with his stripes we are healed." Isaiah 53:5

This continued daily for about fourteen months. When someone asked, "Are you OK?" I took the confession of the Shunammite woman who confessed in the face of death, "It is well" (2 Kings 4:8-37). On an annual visit to the doctor more tests were run. The Hepatitis B was no where to be found. I resisted the devil's plague with the Word of God even though it was evident that he had come to destroy me (James 4:7). God, through Jesus Christ, rebuked the devourer for my sake and I was healed.

For a long time, I found myself embarrassed to talk of this testimony. The devil made me feel ashamed that I had ever been plagued with hepatitis B. This was not a fault of mine or was it? I can imagine how legions of demons gather around someone with

AIDS, cancer and other diseases to shame them out of their blessings. Demons try to condemn them with accusations of sin that makes them believe that they should not go forth to claim their healing. Thank God that the woman with the issue of blood to receive healing took the risk of being exposed. Greater still, thank God that he exposed such a private healing of this woman to us through His Word that we can find courage to be healed and help a brother or sister towards the one who does everything but fail. That person is Jesus Christ. This woman so virtuously illustrated how healing is our right as Christians! God made a promise not to put any diseases upon us because he wants to heal us. (Ex. 15:26)

If you are not a Christian and have a blood disease sapping your life away, get saved! The same miracle working power that healed her and healed me will heal you. There is healing in your reaching out to touch Jesus. This woman proved to us through her testimony that even if we do not know Him but are desperate enough to reach out believing that all things are possible, Jesus will take notice, heal you and use you for His glory. If you have trouble reaching out to Jesus, go to a local assembly or contact someone that you know to be a Christian and ask them about salvation. Ask them to direct you in the Word of God concerning healing. And, learn to believe God at His Word.

PORTRAIT NINE

"A Queen With An Unfavorable Past"

BATHSHEBA

AKA BATHSHUA

II Sam. 11:2-12:24; I Kings 1:11-31; 2:13-19

I Chron. 3:5; II Sam. 23:34, 39

Although in the introduction of this book Bathsheba was mentioned, she is also befitting to close our look into a choice few portraits of virtuous women from the Word of God. We have looked at only a few of the women, who were more than likely to be excommunicated, stoned, or deemed too tainted for holy service unto God by the Church. Yet, these women have left behind great victory trails of faith to follow for anyone who needs to know the way to obtain virtuous victory through the promises of God's Word.

Once while attending a "Women of Excellence" meeting, the speaker posed a question to the group. The question was,

"Who are some of your most favorite women characters in the Bible?"

In ignorance of her life's story, I responded, "Bathsheba." Her name sounded royal and sheik to me. The speaker said to me,

"Later on I will be curious to know why you chose Bathsheba." I was really glad that question never came back around the group. I was not prepared to answer it. Today, admitting that she is still one of my most favorite women characters in the Bible makes me nervous. Only because when I look into her portrait, I can see a glimpse of my own character. I am confronted with my not so perfect past and my struggles to become all that God has predestined me to be. I look at a character such as Queen Esther and wonder what it is like to have been so noble all through life. But, thank God for the open life portrait of Queen Bathsheba, whose life triumphed over immorality. No! We cannot change the past but we can have a future! Queen Bathsheba's portrait reassures us that God can and will take our past, put it behind us, and bestow upon us royalty as His daughters.

It is difficult to tell Bathsheba's story without mentioning, in detail, her husband King David. Scriptures related to their marriage relationship are listed above for your reference. Take the opportunity to read and explore their life further. However, focus will be centered on Bathsheba's character and experiences pertaining to the adversities of her life, her restoration as a God fearing woman, and her contribution to the Kingdom of God.

What were Bathsheba's experiences before meeting the king?

Bathsheba's father, Eliam was a military man (II Sam. 11:3; 23:34). Like any father, Eliam proudly watched his daughter blossom into a very beautiful young woman. He watched over her with careful protection. One could infer that Eliam chose his daughter's first husband, Uriah. They both served in the military of King David's army and had the opportunity to get to know each other (II Sam. 23:39). He grew fond of Uriah because he was probably a man after his own heart. Approving of him and knowing him to be a man of integrity, he took Uriah home to meet his lovely daughter Bathsheba. The two became husband and wife.

No one knows how long they were married. We can summate they were a young couple. Perhaps almost newlyweds by the fresh recall of one, when King David inquired of her, as being Uriah's wife (II Sam. 11:3). We know that her husband was sent off to war before they had any children. This leads us to believe that there was very little time for marital bliss between the two of them prior to his going to war. One could imagine Bathsheba's greatest fear to be Uriah walking out the door, being killed during the war, and never returning home. There was no way she could have imagined that her husband's death would have something to do with her.

What involved Bathsheba in her husband's death?

"And it came to pass in an evening tide, that David arose from off his bed, and walked upon the roof of the king's house: and from the roof he saw a woman washing herself; and the woman was very beautiful to look upon." II Sam 11:2

The scripture mentioned above indicates that King David's palace overlooked most of the land. He could see activities hidden from the normal view from there. It all started with a bath to purify herself. Bathsheba, according to their custom, would have been bathing herself in a place hidden away from the eyes of others. Taking an evening stroll and looking over the city, King David saw Bathsheba bathing. The scriptures do not indicate that Bathsheba was on a roof bathing. King David was on the roof. This is when his lustful passions ignited into flaming desire to have her.

(v3) And David sent and enquired after the woman. And one said, Is not this Bathsheba, the daughter of Eliam, the wife of Uriah the Hittite? (v4) And David sent messengers, and took her; and she came in unto him, and he lay with her; for she was purified from her uncleanness: and she returned unto her house. II Sam. 11:3-4

While her husband served faithfully in the king's army, Bathsheba was drafted into adultery. It is not known whether she had a choice to turn him down. The king summoned her and the scripture says **he took her**. Abraham thought it possible on two separate occasions that the kings he encountered, because of Sarah's beauty, was capable of killing him. This led him to deny their marriage in order to save his life. Abraham relied on his covenant with God to deal with the kings involved and his wife was restored to him untouched (Gen. 12:11-20; 20:1-18). This was not the case with Uriah's wife Bathsheba.

King David was the man in covenant with God and all the men respected him and feared to trespass against him. The favor of God upon him was so great that He divided and conquered the land with great victories. This afforded him extreme confidence in his army's ability to maintain the nation's defense, while he peacefully stayed home and relaxed during this particular time of war. When he inquired about Bathsheba, he was told she was another man's wife. This did not stop him from sending for her and no man dared rebuke him for the sin he was about to commit. We only guess that Bathsheba did not respond as humbly as Tamar did when her brother Amnon raped her (Portrait #6). We have no record of the conversation that took place between them. How do you respond to the great king of all Israel in such a matter? Perhaps, she was even flattered that the king desired her. I do not believe that she wanted her husband killed. One thing is for sure; he used his royal authority to have his way with her. After his evening of indulging in passions of lust, he returned her to her home with a royal decree to never mention the event to anyone. But this sin threatened exposure without her ever mumbling a word. She was pregnant by the king.

> (v5) And the woman conceived, and sent and told David, and said, I am with child.

Bathsheba was caught up in uncontrollable iniquities that threatened her life. She and her husband had not been together in months. There was no way to lie her way out of this death penalty sin that the king had thrust upon her. Surely, the law of the land would have put her to death. One of the Ten Commandments had been broken, **Thou shalt not commit adultery**. The penalty would require that both the man and the woman be put to death.

> "And that man that committeth adultery with another man's wife, even he that committeth adultery with his neighbor's wife, the adulterer and the adulteress shall surely be put to death." Lev. 20:10

The king would not have been put to death unless God Himself imposed the penalty. Bathsheba, on the other hand, would have suffered the loss of her life. Fearing the consequences of this sin, Bathsheba sent word to the king that she was pregnant. Who else could she turn to? All of society would have condemned her except the one who was guilty of transgressing against her marriage. She did not know what to think or expect. Would he turn against her? Would he leave her alone to face this situation? Would he deny ever having been with her? She had no other alternative but to turn to the one responsible for the situation. Engulfed with anxiety and fear, she awaited his response.

How did the King respond to the news of her pregnancy?

Scriptures do not reveal whether he communicated further with Bathsheba how he was going to handle the situation. He first made two attempts to resolve the matter with a cover up by bringing her husband home off the battlefield. This would give him the opportunity to be with his wife and become a proud father.

> (v6) And David sent to Joab, saying, Send me Uriah the Hittite. And Joab sent Uriah to David. (v7) And when Uriah was come unto him, David demanded of him how Joab did, and how the people did, and how the war prospered. (v8) And David said to Uriah, Go down to thy house, and wash thy feet. And Uriah departed out of the king's house, and there followed him a mess of meat from the king. (v9) But Uriah slept at the door of the king's house with all the servants of his lord, and went not down to his house. II Sam. 11:6-9

King David knew that Uriah was a man of military integrity, commitment, and skills. Uriah ranked among the top thirty-seven of King David's mighty men. With intent to inflate Uriah's ego, the king tried flattering him into thinking that his military opinion was most valued by the king and that there existed some close and endeared relationship between them. He inquired about the other military commanders and the status of the war. He assumed that Uriah would feel privileged to have earned a night with his beautiful wife because of the king's gratitude. Like a father wanting to give his son rest, the king ordered him **Go to your house, and wash thy feet**. He further supplied a feast for Uriah and his wife's night of intimate reunion. His assumptions were wrong! Uriah would not go home.

134

Uriah confessed to the king that his respect for his covenant responsibility as an officer before the ark of God, Israel, and Judah, his higher-ranking officer Joab, the people and even the king, himself would not allow him to indulge in fleshly gratification. He made a vow, **as thou livest, and as thy soul liveth, I will not do this thing (v11)**. The king made one more attempt to manipulate Uriah into going home to be with his wife.

> (v12) And David said to Uriah, Tarry here today also, and tomorrow I will let thee depart. So Uriah abode in Jerusalem that day, and the morrow. (v13) And when David had called him, he did eat and drink before him; he went out to lie on his bed with the servants of his lord, but went not down to his house. II Sam. 11:12-13

Even under the influence of alcohol, Uriah remained true to his vow. He never considered going home. Three days had passed since Bathsheba had received the feast addressed to both husband and wife with compliments from the king. But her husband had not yet walked through the door. She must have been sick with fear and worry of not knowing what was taking place between the king and her husband. What could she do? Nothing! Not one thing! She could not undo the bathing situation...

She could not roll back the clock and take back whatever part she must have played in this whole ordeal. She knew that no good thing could happen at this point. The king had moved to his final plan. That plan was a decree that would secure his success in taking care of the problem.

What was the decree?

King David's actions in dealing with Uriah proved Abraham's fears of the lawless attitude of a king in his lust for another man's wife, to be true. A more unbearable truth; Bathsheba's greatest fear was about to turn into an even greater real life nightmare that she could not wake up from. King David, the man she was pregnant by, the supreme ruler of the land, ruthlessly decreed Uriah's death, unknowingly carried by his own hands to the executor.

> (v 14) And it came to pass in the morning, that David wrote a letter to Joab and sent it by the hand of Uriah. (v15) And he wrote in the letter, saying, Set ye Uriah in the forefront of the hottest battle, and retire ye from him, that he may be smitten, and die. (v16) And it came to pass, when Joab observed the city, that he assigned Uriah unto a place where he knew that valiant men were. (v17) And the men of the city went out, and fought with Joab: and there fell some of the people of the servants of David; and Uriah the Hittite died also. II Sam. 11:14-17

King David was now relieved that Uriah was dead. It did not matter that another one of his devout officer, Abimelech, was killed in the process of his cover-up. He sent this message to Joab,

> (v25) Then David said unto the messenger, Thus shalt thou say unto Joab, Let not this thing displease thee, for the sword devoureth one as well as another: make thy battle more strong against the city, and overthrow it: and encourage thou him. II Sam 11:25

It was finished. Now he would wait for the appropriate time of mourning to pass and take Bathsheba to be his wife.

How did Bathsheba take all of this?

"And when the wife of Uriah heard that Uriah her husband was dead, she mourned for her husband." II Sam. 11: 26

Though mourning was a formal ceremony performed during this era, I believe that Bathsheba genuinely mourned the loss of her husband. Especially since the next scripture says in part, **But the thing that David had done displeased the Lord (v27).** God contributed this sin to David. When one perpetuates sin, all are affected by it. The guilty and the guiltless suffer alike. If Bathsheba had used in anyway seduction, or persuasive words to cause this tare in the covenant relationship between God and David or have her husband killed, would her deeds not be recorded in the Word?

When Eve seduced Adam into eating of the forbidden fruit, the part she played in the fall of man was recorded (Gen. 3:12-13). When Jezebel plotted to kill Naboth for a vineyard to give to her husband and to kill Elijah, the prophet because of his victory over the prophets of Baal, her deeds were recorded (I King 21; I King 19:1-3). When Herodias plotted to kill John the Baptist to cover up her unlawful marriage to her Uncle Phillip's brother, the truth was recorded (Matt. 14:3-12). And in Bathsheba's case the truth was recorded. She did mourn for her husband. King David did not share the details of what he was going to do, but Bathsheba knew that her husband's death was because of the king's lust for her.

This made her mourning even more grievous. Still Bathsheba had to live on with the consequences of sin.

What were the consequences she experienced?

"And when the mourning was past, David sent and fetched her to his house, and she became his wife, and bare him a son. But the thing that David had done displeased the Lord." II Sam. 11:27

This was a very stressful and difficult time for Bathsheba. Within a few short months, she had gone from being newly married, to being drafted into adultery, to being pregnant by a man who had supreme authority over the land. Notwithstanding, she had become a widow and now married to the man who was responsible for it all. The comforts of the palace may have added some physical sense of future safety and security, but mentally Bathsheba was in turmoil. She was just added to his collection of wives that had at one time also captured the king's heart. There was hardly any time to think about mental pains. Bathsheba was just a few months into the palace when the labor pains of her first child demanded all of her attention.

"A woman when she is in travail hath sorrow, because her hour is come: but as soon as she is delivered of the child, she remembereth no more the anguish, for joy that a man is born into the world. "John 16:21

There she endured the pain. Hours of travailing passed the day until she gave birth to a healthy baby boy. The pain was now over. Now she could rest. At first sight, she could see the perfect beauty and innocence of her first born son. It was time to put everything else behind her. Now was the time for her to allow healing to begin physically, mentally, and spiritually.

Bathsheba had no idea that the rest from her delivery pains and grief would be momentarily.

What caused Bathsheba's rest to be temporal?

Bathsheba awakened after a few hours of rest to more agony and grief. She did not know that in private, Nathan, the prophet had just spoken to the king in judgment. The life of her newborn child had been required as the ultimate penalty for the king's sin.

> (v9) Wherefore hast thou despised the commandment of the Lord, to do evil in his sight? thou has killed Uriah the Hittite with the sword, and hast taken his wife to be thy wife, and hast slain him with the sword of the children of Ammon.(v14) Howbeit, because by this deed thou hast given great occasion to the enemies of the Lord to blaspheme, the child also that is born unto thee shall surely die. (v15) And Nathan departed unto his house. And the Lord struck the child that Uriah's wife bare unto David, and it was very sick.

> (v16) David therefore besought God for the child; and David fasted, and went in, and lay all night upon the earth. (v17) And the elders of his house arose, and went to him to raise him up from the earth: but he would not, neither did he eat bread with them. (18) And it came to pass on the seventh day, that the child died. And the servants of David feared to tell him that the child was dead: for they said, Behold, while the child was yet alive, we spake unto him, and he would not hearken unto our voice: how will he then vex himself, if we tell him that the child is dead? II Sam. 12:9, 14-18

We can picture the grievous torment King David experienced during the seven days the child's life had begun to depart from him. His anguish was clearly described to us.

As for Bathsheba, her sufferings had to be beyond words. Had she been told the prophecy concerning the child while he was living? It would not have made a difference. For seven long days and nights, she had to walk through the valley of the shadow of death. Then death claimed her innocent child's life. Like many of us, Bathsheba probably asked the question, Why so much pain?

Why did God allow so much pain into Bathsheba's life?

The life of Bathseba can be seen as that of one foreshadowing the life of Mary, the mother of our Saviour. While in a covenant relationship to be married to Joseph and still a virgin, Mary became pregnant by the Holy Spirit of God (Matt. 1:18-21). The truth of how she became pregnant and the reason for it appeared to the world to be a lie and out of order. God judged sin and provided the promise of redemption. Mary's child would be born into the world to die for the sins of all mankind. Mary had received the following prophecy when she went to present her first born son in the temple:

> (v34) And Simeon blessed them, and said unto Mary his mother, Behold, this child is set for the fall and rising again of many in Israel; and for a sign which shall be spoken against; (v35) (Yea, a sword shall pierce through thy own soul also,) that the thoughts of many hearts may be revealed. Luke 2:34-35

In like manner this prophecy resembles the pain endured by Bathsheba as her child's death foreshadowed the redemptive promise of the holy child, Jesus, who would die for our sins. King David was in a special covenant relationship with God. Christ, the promised Saviour, would be born of his family descendants (II Sam. 23:5). This covenant would grant mankind eternal mercy at repentance by taking away his guilt of sins and placing it upon the innocent.

God initiated and established this covenant agreement by His word. He penalized His own innocent Son's life, to spare the guilty man once and for all, and for the life of all mankind (Heb. 9:11- 15). The divine covenant of redemption was fulfilled by Christ dying on the Cross for all of our sins but not before God redeemed King David's life back from sin through innocent blood.

> "For the wages of sin is death; but the gift of God is eternal life through Jesus Christ our Lord." Romans 6:23

The promised redemption would no longer require the blood sacrifice of animals. A new and better covenant was to be established through the throne of King David. The life of King David and Bathsheba's child paid the price for them to live and thereby preserved the progressive covenant of redemption for all mankind. Living under the covenant of law, David and Bathsheba should have been put to death. Christ, the promised Saviour, God's Son had not yet came and died to take away our sins. In order for God to preserve his plan of salvation for the world and show forth his mercy, he foreshadowed his eternal gift of life through the death of his Son, by the death of David's son. This was done because King David's throne was to be established forever and the Saviour was to come from his kingdom. God preserved his life to preserve His promise to all mankind (Ps. 89:34-36). If God had assessed the penalty of death to King David, the divine plan of redemption would have been aborted. Therefore, God judged it and assessed the penalty of death to King David's son just as He would His own Son, Jesus Christ. God did not spare His own Son and this child's death for his parents sin, was symbolic in reference to what was going to take place in the future through Jesus Christ for the world. Bathsheba came to know that same sword piercing her soul that Mary would endure through her son's death on the Cross so that others could live.

How does Bathsheba triumph through all her trials?

Bathsheba was a queen with scars from the past and although she had scars from the past, she was still a queen. She was a great one at best. The consequences of sin and circumstances railroaded Bathsheba into this position. No one likes to think of a great person as being a common person with abominable stains of sin, or as being called to do something great for God. It somehow dilutes our perfect image of them and causes us to not recognize their significant contributions to the overall sustaining of life. Former First Lady, Hillary Clinton is a prime example of how we minimize significant contributions all because we associate a person with detestable sins of their own or someone else's.

The following statements are not intended to be political in nature but to relate to an American Queen (First Lady) who experience public trials concerning her marriage and how she triumphed through her struggles. Most all Americans are familiar with some of the trials that Former First Lady Hillary Rodham Clinton experienced while serving alongside her husband- Former President of the United States, Bill Clinton. If society could look past any personal prejudices and stone casting, they would see that Former First Lady Clinton proved herself to be unselfish in her political aspirations to serve the public. Her desire to develop a public standard that would defend the rights of children and families is what motivated her to pursue public office. Thus, in Arkansas, she founded a home-based program that would enhance the quality of education in economically challenged homes. As she served alongside of her husband, she demonstrated what the backbone of a family and commitment to our nation should be, by not bowing down under pressure. However, all during their presidential service to the United States, Former First Lady Clinton experienced constant accusations of immoral character. Tabloids accused her of being a lesbian. They printed bold front pages involving her daughter, Chelsea. And, society has continued to scandalize her reputation. These piercing daggers aimed target at the heart and soul of Mrs. Clinton and intended to destroy her life's calling, her family, and the demoralization of her character. But, she would have none of that!

Whether all of the accusations were true or not, Former First Lady Clinton was not going to let the devil into her family to destroy what God had ordained! When her husband's affair with Monica Lewinsky became a public scandal across the nations, she refused to let her husband's affair with a younger woman abort her family's destiny. She acted pretty much like Sarah did in preserving Isaac's covenant inheritance by putting Abraham's concubine Hagar, with her son Ishmael, out because they threatened to take away the promised blessings (Gen. 16, 21). Not once did Sarah think about giving up Abraham or their destiny. Mrs. Clinton stood in her place of ordination and refused to be moved. She would not buckle under fear, pain, torment, depression, discouragement, guilt or disgust! There was no time to wallow in self-pity. The preserving

143

of her marital rights was at stake right then. Their enemies mean spirited accusations, continues even until this day. But, because she would not bow down, I believe that God took the accusations against her family and rendered them of non-effect; just like God did with the accusations of Satan when he stood against Joshua, the high priest, before God.

> (v1) And he shewed me Joshua the high priest standing before the angel of the Lord, and Satan standing at his right hand to resist him. (v2) And the Lord said unto Satan, The Lord rebuke them O Satan; even the Lord that hath chosen Jerusalem rebuke thee: is not this a brand plucked out of the fire? (v3) Now Joshua was clothed with filthy garments, and stood before the angel. (v4) And he answered and spake unto those that stood before him, saying, Take away the filthy garments from him. And unto him he said, Behold, I have caused thine iniquity to pass from thee, and I will clothe thee with change of raiment. (v5) And I said, Let them set a fair mitre upon his head. So they set a fair mitre upon his head, and clothed him with garments. And the angel of the Lord stood by. (v6) And the angel of the Lord protested unto Joshua, saying,

> (v7) Thus saith the Lord of hosts; if thou wilt walk in my ways, and if thou wilt keep my charge, then thou shalt also judge my house, and shalt also keep my courts, and I will give thee places to walk among these that stand by. Zechariah 3:1

Indeed, God did set a mitre, a headdress of leadership, upon Former First Lady Clinton's head. Shortly thereafter, she was blessed with favor among the people and went on to win the Office

144

of Senator for the state of New York. She continues in honorary service to and for the welfare of the people. Former President Clinton and her daughter Chelsea no doubt will honor her and call her blessed. All Americans will remember that she did not tuck tail and run for a safe place to hide or console her pains. She rose like the mother eagle in protecting her nest. Responding any other way to her trials and tribulations would have caused the Clinton Administration to fold in disgrace. In addition, her marriage would possibly have failed. Chelsea, their daughter, would perhaps have experienced some severe and practically irreversible mental damages, and any future political aspirations Mrs. Clinton may have had would have been aborted. Her family would have been torn apart and the administration brought to utter shame. In like manner, Bathsheba rose to the standard of a virtuous queen.

Survival for Bathsheba meant that she would rise to the occasion of becoming King David's Queen. Bathsheba was very common but the position of Queen was Royal. Circumstances determined her position in life but God placed her in this position by divine appointment, just as he did Mary, the mother of Jesus, and Hillary Clinton, a Presidential First Lady. God knew that Bathsheba would endure the pain, keep her testimony and teach diligently the fear and holy reverence of God.

Bathsheba was faced with many choices that would determine her fate in the palace. Simultaneously, she was experiencing devastating losses and pains in her life. Despite all that took place, Bathsheba found favor in the eyes of King David and God.

King David did not respond to God about her as Adam did with Eve when he fell in the Garden of Eden (Gen. 3:10-12). Nor, did King David put her away out of his sight behind his lust driven sins for her that caused him to receive harsh punishment from the hand of God. In as much as, Kings often responded that way when they were no longer pleased with the woman (Esther 2:13-14). God appeared to have placed extraordinary favor over Bathsheba's life with King David. As soon as the customary purification was over, King David went in unto her to console her grief.

> (v24) And David comforted Bathsheba his wife, and went into unto her, and lay with her: and she bare a son, and he called his name Solomon: and the Lord loved him. (v25) And he (God) sent by the hand of Nathan the prophet; and he called his name Jedidiah (Beloved of God), because of the Lord. II Sam.12:24-25

God blessed the fruit of her womb and she gave birth to Solomon, the wisest man that ever lived outside of Christ. Though Bathsheba was the last formal wife of King David's to be mentioned, she moved with wisdom to ensure that her son, Solomon, would be blessed to carry on the covenant throne that his father, King David, had with God. It is evident that Bathsheba was a God fearing woman and knew the voice of God speaking through the prophet (I Kings 1:15-21). With the same prophet, Nathan, that God spoke a death word over her first son, she received instructions for the life of her second son to preserve the covenant promise. God's favor upon Bathsheba placed Solomon upon the throne of his father, King David.

> (v28) Then king David answered and said, Call me Bathsheba. And she came into the king's presence, and stood before the king. (v29) And the king sware, and said, As the Lord liveth, that hath redeemed my soul out of all distress, (v30) Even as I sware unto thee by the Lord God of Israel, saying, Assuredly

Solomon thy son shall reign after me, and he shall sit upon my throne in my stead; even so will I certainly do this day. (v31) Then Bathsheba bowed with her face to the earth, and did reverence to the king, and said, Let my lord king David live forever. I Kings 1:28-31

All throughout the Proverbs, Solomon, this very son that God loved, wrote in acknowledgement of his mother's wisdom and instructions. He believed her counsel to have had significantly influenced his and his father's life greatly, as well as, her counsel would be a life giving resource guide for others. His wise sayings admonished the reader and hearers of God's Word to reverence their mother and to hear and yield to the voice of her wisdom. He relates it this way,

"My son, hear the instruction of thy father, and forsake not the law of thy mother." Prov. 1:8

"My son, keep thy father's commandment, and forsake not the law of thy mother." Prov. 6:20

"Every wise woman buildeth her house: but the foolish plucketh it down with her hands." Prov. 14:1

"A wise son maketh a glad father: but a foolish man despiseth his mother." Prov. 15:20

"Whoso curseth his father or his mother, his lamp shall be put out in obscure darkness." Prov. 20:20

"He then hammers it home to us in this manner, Hearken unto thy father that begat thee, and despise not thy mother when she is old." Prov. 23:22

Certainly, King Solomon cherished the training of his mother and when she was old, he despised her not. Nor, did he disregard her wisdom, courage, or faithfulness to the royal kingdom that represented God's Kingdom. In honoring her, King Solomon bowed with respect and sat his mother, Bathsheba, at his right side whenever she entered the throne room.

> "Bathsheba therefore went unto king Solomon, to speak unto him for Adonijah. And the king rose up to meet her, and bowed himself unto her, and sat down on his throne, and caused a seat to be set for the king's mother; and she sat on his right hand." I Kings 2:19

Truly, we can see in Bathsheba's life that she excelled all of the other queens before her. Abigail, in example, did virtuously when she moved to save her whole house from destruction by the hand of King David and was given the same honor of becoming his queen (I Sam. 25:1-42). However, her son, Chileab, was not bestowed the honor of his father's throne. Nor, did Abigail have anymore children by the king. On the other hand, God opened Bathsheba's womb and she gave birth to five sons of King David (2 Chron. 3:5). She remained the king's favorite wife until his death. Her son, Solomon, honored her and patterned his wise sayings in the book of Proverbs in acknowledgement of her character; and primarily she inhabited the favor of God. God esteemed her high above the rest of the queens because she endured the pain, kept her testimony, and taught diligently the fear of the Lord.

PORTRAIT TEN

The Virtuous Woman God Called "Me" To Be

_____

Place your name here

Reference Scripture:

Living Testimony Currently Being Recorded In the Book of Life

Rev. 3:5-6

(v5) He that overcometh, the same shall be clothed in white raiment; and I will not blot out his name out of the book of life, but I will confess his name before my Father, and before his angels (v6) He that hath an ear, let him hear what the Spirit saith unto the churches.

What do we have to overcome?

In the previous chapters the women portrayed are in no wise a complete representation of the women of the Bible who overcame flaws within their character, oppressing situations, and circumstances. They represent only a few of the many women who rose to victorious living in Biblical days through seemingly impossible situations. Prayerfully, you have become more acquainted with some of the diversified trials that women inside and outside of the Body of Christ have faced and are still facing.

This book was written to help in the recognition that there are no "unique" struggles when one is coming out of the world into a holy and virtuous lifestyle, living in Christ Jesus. However, there are unique individuals, who are extremely important to God. He has a divine plan of restoration through Jesus Christ for every individual person, regardless of their life's trials. God will honor our confessions before the world, as well as, the desires of our hearts, just as he did each and everyone of the Biblical women portrayed in this book. They all had "real life" issues to overcome and Christians today (especially women) are still facing the same.

Past and present struggles have many Christian women in great denial and in hiding. Mainly afraid of the criticism they may face from the church, they don't want to appear unholy. Nearly all of the women recorded within the Word of God had a testimony of struggling through issues. Today, Christian women are familiar with those very same issues. They are being affected by them in their everyday living over two thousand years later. Let us recap a moment:

1. **Eve** - We are reminded that all of creation fell into sin because of her seduction towards her husband. However, Eve confessed her sin and repented. God did not kill her, nor did He replace her with another wife for Adam. After all was said and done, God spoke His sovereign destiny over Eve's life, **I will put enmity between thee and the woman, and between thy seed and her seed; it shall bruise thy head, and thou shalt bruise his heel** (Gen. 3:15). Satan would not have another opportunity to deceive her again and her seed would grow up to have victory over her enemy. Thus, Eve fulfilled her preeminent calling as mother of all mankind.

2. **Deborah** - A woman spiritually ordained to judge all Israel, to proclaim words of truth by the gift of prophecy, and ordered victorious battle strategies in a time when the voice of women was inappropriate and unappreciated. Deborah did not have any recognizable sins but her courage should be admired. She was courageous for accepting the call of leadership by God during such an era. She endured cultural discrimination against women. Even though she commanded the war to victory through Barak; the victory of the battle went to another woman, by the name of, Jael. Nevertheless, Deborah never thought about giving up the fight. Jael did a good thing by killing the captain of the enemy's army. But, Deborah excelled all the men and women of her day by becoming the mouthpiece of God in unfavorable times. Thus, a whole nation was delivered from 20 years of oppression through the divine call of God upon her life.

3. **Rahab** - There was no virtuosity in the way Rehab lived her life as a well-known harlot in the city of Jericho. It would have appeared that she was stuck in this degrading profession for the rest of her life. She was hell bound with no redemption in sight. Who could take her sins away and give her a new life? God, Almighty, was the only one that could and He did just that! The walls of Jericho came down. So did the strongholds of Rahab's life. Rehab was saved and blessed to the utmost. God destroyed a whole city but saved only Rahab and her family because she entered into covenant with Him and His people. God did not stop with just saving her. He used her life to bring forth descendants that His darling Son, Our Savior Jesus Christ, would come through promising redemption to all that call on His name.

4. **Jael** - "Blessed above women shall Jael the wife of Heber the Kenite be, blessed shall she be above women in the tent." The prophetess Deborah sung this praise of Jael. The significance of this praise towards her was not that she took a life. A life without God is already condemned (Jo. 3:18). The heart of this praise is lodged within the fact that she utterly destroyed the enemy out of her life and the life of God's people. The enemy's oppression would not get a second chance to rise up again in her life or the life of others. God praised Jael through the lips of Deborah for taking a strong stand against sin and restored her family to the fellowship of God's people.

5. **Leah** - And he [Jacob] went in also unto Rachel, and he loved also Rachel more than Leah, and served with him yet seven other years. (v31) And when the Lord saw that Leah was hated, he opened her womb: But Rachel was barren (Gen. 29:30-31). Whether it was her less favorable countenance or her age, Leah's father engaged in a deceitful ploy to marry her off to a man in love with his younger daughter, Rachel. Because of her father's trickery, no matter how hard Leah struggled to prove her trustworthiness and love, she could never win her husband's love or her sister's respect. She loved him, bore him children, one after another, yet she remained unloved. The blessedness of Leah's story is that no matter how deep the hurt was or bitter the scorns of her husband and sister became, she did not allow herself to become bitter, vengeful, or wallow in self pity. She used the only weapon that could have triumphed through such rejection and that was unconditional love. Therefore, Leah reaped the love of God and his comfort. God would not go against Jacob's love for Rachel but he did comfort Leah by giving her children. More importantly, God honored her praises. Leah and her sons were able to be counted

as blessed by God when He established an eternal covenant with all of Jacob's sons -The Twelve Tribes of Israel.

6. **Tamar** - Tamar's story represents the struggles of women who have been violated. Tamar was born a beautiful princess. The disgraceful fact that she was raped by her half-brother made her tear off her royal robe and denounce all of the promises of her father's kingdom, **And Tamar put ashes on her head, and rent her garment of divers colors that was on her; and laid her hand on her head, and went on crying** (II Sam.13:19). But, all of the self-punishment, denial of self worth, and isolation did not change the fact that Tamar was the king's daughter. She had the right to still claim all of her father's blessings. No matter what trials life has dealt you, as God's princess, you are still entitled to all of His Kingdom blessings. After being raped, Tamar lived for her time period, a virtuous and an honorable life. However, she chose to remain unfruitful because of her pain. God does not want you to be unfruitful. He will heal you, love you, and bless you with an abundant life (Jo. 10:10).

7. **The Woman of Samaria** - How many Christian women would admit that they can identify with this woman's life? She was abreast of the Word, **The woman saith unto him, I know that Messias commeth, which is called the Christ: when he is come, he will tell us all things** (Jo. 4:25). But, this did not prevent the breakdown of her relationships. She had five husbands and was living with a man when she met Jesus. Five failed marriages was a sure way for a woman, in those days, to be branded unfit for a proper covenant marriage. Most certainly today, she would be an embarrassing thorn among holy women in the church. But, how many "church" women have had more than five lovers for any length of time? If Jesus had met anyone of us at the well, how many

husbands would he tell us we have had? The good news is, when she asked for the **"living water"** that he had made available, Jesus addressed her concerns. Her story ends with her worshiping Him in Spirit and in truth. By her testimony, she became virtuous leading (evangelizing) her city to Christ.

8. **The Woman With An Issue of Blood** - A dying woman who reached out for life. In unbelief, she could have allowed Jesus to pass her by. She could have reasoned with herself why she shouldn't be healed but she did not choose to entertain doubting thoughts. Once she heard about Jesus, the coming Messiah, she became virtuous by never doubting her right to receive healing as a Kingdom daughter. This woman possessed more than hope. She had confidence in her faith. And, that faithful confidence made her know she could and would be healed by just reaching out to touch Jesus anywhere. Her situation boasted death to her heart, just as loudly as, any of the terminal diseases present today boast to the heart of their victims. This woman resisted the roar of death. She refused to submit to its fear, torment, and phobias. This plain, ordinary woman's testimony, makes her a champion because she grabbed hold of her faith for life. Healing belongs to you! What will you do with her testimony and the Word of God?

9. **Bathsheba** - No matter the trial, no matter the heartache, this woman virtuously kept the testimony of God in her mouth. Sin barged its destructive pathway into her life through King David's lust for her and left behind a massive trail of chaos. The filth of adultery and a bloody trail of murder caused divine judgment and the death of their innocent child. However, Bathsheba accepted the sovereign decision of God in this matter. If God had taken the life of the two of them in punishment for their sin, what would have happened to the redemptive covenant that would have come from

King David's family tree? Often, people who have experienced this magnitude of trauma in their life, resolve that God does not care about them. They either stop trusting Him or become very angry and bitter with God for what He has allowed to come into their lives. Bathsheba resolved within herself that there is only one way in life and that is God's way. Therefore, the same God that punished was able to bless. Bathsheba kept going, looking, and expecting the blessings of God. Her latter days were extremely blessed of the Lord. Because of her enduring faithfulness to God, we have the wisdom of life through the Book of Proverbs written by her son, King Solomon. In addition, she became the most favorable queen in King David's throne and much, much more.

10. The Woman God Called You to Be

"Many daughters have done virtuously, but thou excellest them all." Proverbs 31:29

What has God called me to do?

Of all the women you can relate to in His Word, God has called you to excel above them all. If you can relate to the life story of Rahab, God is calling you to have a greater faith to believe that He will do whatever necessary to deliver you, save you, and bless you. If you can relate to the life story of Tamar, God does not expect you to live in isolation for the rest of your life. He wants you to expect a more abundant life from Him. If you can relate to the woman with the issue of blood; God not only wants you to rise up and be healed, but also to be able to lay hands on the sick, so that they may recover. Although, there are no examples of women in prison, all of these women were in a bondage that held them captive. God wants you to be free in mind, spirit, body, and soul. What is the first step towards my virtuous image?

155

What is the first step towards my virtuous image?

Behold your natural self in the mirror...

(v22) But be ye doers of the word, and not hearers only, deceiving your own selves. (v23) For if any be a hearer of the word, and not a doer, he is like unto a man beholding his natural face in a glass: (v24) For he beholdeth himself, and goeth his way, and straightway forgetteth what manner of man he was. James 1:22-24

Take an intimate moment between you, the mirror of your heart, and the Holy Spirit to be alone. Be completely honest with yourself and God. Look past the appearance of self-confidence that you parade before the rest of the world and undress yourself in the spirit. Trust yourself to confide in yourself. What do you see? What issues are you faced with? Are there areas in your life that you need deliverance from? Do you struggle with secret sins and reoccurring habits that you know could bring devastating consequences to your life? God wants us to stop deceiving ourselves and to forgive ourselves.

All sins are not classified in the category of abominable to man. But, to God, sin is a loathsome smell in His nostrils. Perhaps, you gossip too much or maybe, you are too passive about life. Maybe, you are a compulsive spender when shopping which causes you to be financially oppressed or non-supportive of your spiritual home. Maybe, you live in a constant state of condemnation over past failures, preventing you from believing **you can do all things through Christ which strengthens you** (Phil 4:13). Perhaps, life has beaten you up so bad, you cannot see any hope beyond your present circumstances. You need God to show you the way to a more abundant life. I must admit, when I did this (looked in the mirror at myself) a few years ago, I felt anything but virtuous. Before I knew virtuous qualities existed in me, the devil, through life's trails, had seemingly raped me of all my treasures. In all honesty, perhaps you feel yourself also to be anything but virtuous. Has life raped you of all your innocence and virtuous qualities, causing you to conform to a general existence in life? God wants to introduce you to an abundant life and his perfect law of liberty.

What is the law of liberty?

"But whoso looketh into the perfect law of liberty, and continueth therein, he being not a forgetful hearer, but a doer of the work, this man shall be blessed in his deed." James 1:25

One of Webster's definitions for liberty is an action going beyond normal limits. Applied within the Christian context, one may define liberty as, the freedom to come out of a confined state of being that limits one from reaching their ordained potential in life through the application of faith and the power of the Holy Spirit. This is regardless of the limitations imposed by life's trials and circumstances.

How can liberty help me?

Liberty will free your attitude from the limitations of your past and current trials and encourage your hope with expectations to walk in a new life. God will not do the work for you. He will, however, provide you with the necessary ability to accomplish your new life in Him. Call Jesus over the discouraging echoes of your trials.

Your trials will try to discourage you through the voice of the enemy. The enemy will try to tell you:

- ❖ You can't make it! You will never be anything! You're dumb, stupid, ignorant, and crazy! You are guilty of horrible sins! Jesus won't forgive you! Nor will he heal you! Jesus does not care about you!

- ❖ The devil is a liar! Jesus came and died so that any sin that could ever be committed could be forgiven. His ears are open and waiting to hear our cries over the enemy that tries to discourage us.

- ❖ **The first shall be last and the last shall be first** (Matt 19:30). What a glorious day for you when you decide I don't care how my circumstances boast "dead end", I will call on Jesus, the Master of life, for new life!

Will it be an easy transformation to my new virtuous lifestyle?

No. In your new life, you must learn how to fellowship with Christians and become an active member of the Church. You must learn how to walk in your new liberty of life.

> (v16) Wash you, make you clean; put away the evil of your doings from before mine eyes; cease to do evil; (v17) Learn to do well; seek judgment, relieve the oppressed, judge the fatherless, plead for the widow. (v18) Come now, and let us reason together, saith the Lord: though your sins be as scarlet, they shall be as white as snow; through they be red like crimson, they shall be as wool. (v19) If ye be willing and obedient, ye shall eat the good of the land. Isaiah 1:16-19

God requires us to make a deliberate choice to be cleansed of our sins. Most everyone experiences nakedness in the mirror from time to time. Those are the times in which we see all of our shortcomings. Oftentimes we choose to walk off from the confrontation of our ugliness and choose to forget the naked and embarrassing image we see within ourselves. We even dare others to point our flaws out to us. But before walking away from the truth, we must choose to be washed clean of all our sins.

God will then present us with opportunities to learn and express our new life through a relationship with Him and the Church. As a result, the old sinful nature will become submissive to the victory of Jesus' Cross. The sins of the past will no longer hunt you because you will be confident that He has given you a bright new future without condemnation.

Will I be completely forgiven and accepted into the Church?

> (v3) And being in Bethany in the house of Simon the leper, as he sat at meat, there came a woman having an alabaster box of ointment of spikenard very precious; and she brake the box, and poured it on his head. (v4) And there were some that had indignation within themselves, and said, Why was this waste of the ointment made? (v5) For it might have been sold for more than three hundred pence, and have been given to the poor. And they murmured against her. (v6) And Jesus said, Let her alone; why trouble ye her? She hath wrought a good work on me.

Mark 14:3-9

It is God's desire that you are received with loving and nurturing arms into the Body of Christ. However, the Church is filled with broken people who have come to God for transformation and the transformed life is a lifelong process.

At first, you may have to deal with people in the Church, who have been in Church services all their lives, and do not consider themselves to have ever committed a disgraceful sin. Yet, their heart can be as unloving and judgmental.

You must know within yourself what God has done for you and seek to serve Him with all of your heart and soul. It really does not matter what others think or say about you. Only what Jesus says counts. It is important that you do not have some fairy tale notion of how much easier your life is going to be as you are cultivated by the Holy Spirit into a virtuous woman and fulfill your virtuous calling within the Kingdom of God.

What are the characteristics of a virtuous woman?

There are really no quick and complete definitions of a virtuous woman. An attempt to describe her character would have to be expounded upon from within a broad spectrum of categories. All the books in the world could not describe her in totality. We must grasp the influential truth in which her moral character and strengths are built upon and apply those truths to our lives. The definition rendered in this book is abstracted from the moral fibers of the Word of God and is geared to address the woman who is searching for her way of escape from her own immoralities into the strong, rich, and vibrant virtuous woman God intended. With that thought in mind;

A virtuous woman is a woman who, at some point in life, recognizes that she has not yet reached her full potential in life and needs God to do so. She is willing to take on the responsibility to learn what she does not know. Her spirit is unwilling to submit to defeat as she presses over the mountains of life's cruel adversities and trials. She feeds others in need of her growing wisdom and knowledge in hopes of preventing destruction in their lives. Regardless of who is at fault within a controversy, her actions are prompted to nurture safety, healing, restoration, forgiveness, and deliverance for others. She learns how to act on the behalf and the wellbeing of all parties in a given situation.

There is a plot against your life by Satan. Jesus is the only one that can and has reversed the decree of the enemy against your life. All you have to do is be willing to seek and obey Him. What do you have to loose that you have not already lost without his help?

How do I learn the ways of a virtuous woman?

The book of Proverbs (wise instructions) offers us in depth counseling to correct and enhance our character towards the virtuous standard of God's word. It tells us what we should and should not do. It warns us of the after effects of non-virtuous ways. And, it declares to us the rewards, which result from living virtuously. The woman's ways inspired the writing of the book of Proverbs. The following are a few scriptural admonishments that are characterized of the female traits taken from the counsel of Proverbs:

"Happy is the man that findeth wisdom, and the man that getteth understanding. She is more precious than rubies: and all the things thou canst desire are not to be compared unto her." Prov. 3:13 & 15

"Say unto wisdom, Thou art my sister; and call understanding thy kinswoman." Prov. 7:4

"Wisdom hath builded her house, she hath hewn out her seven pillars". Prov. 9:1

"Wisdom crieth without; she uttereth her voice in the streets." Prov. 1:20

Likewise, we are warned of certain female characteristics:

"To deliver thee from the strange woman, even from the stranger which flattereth with her words. For her house inclineth unto death, and her paths unto the dead." Prov. 2:16 & 18

"For by means of a whorish woman a man is brought to a piece of bread: and the adulteress will hunt for the precious life." Prov. 6:26

"And, behold, there met him a woman with the attire of an harlot, and subtil of heart. Her house is the way to hell, going down to the chambers of death." Prov. 7:10 & 27

The book of Proverbs can, in one way, be interpreted as a complete symbolical dissection of the woman's characteristics. It references the female gender and is called Wisdom due to her complexities, strengths, weaknesses, influences and -- yes, even her destructive abilities. It is written by a man who had 700 wives and 300 concubines.

During his lifelong study of over 1,000 women and overseeing the land, which represented the Kingdom of God, King Solomon noted some remarkable observations of the woman's ability to affect life. These observations represent us whether good or bad. God gave us His Word to live by, to gain knowledge by, and to refer to in the time of trouble. King Solomon's observations along with the Women stories of the Bible, are here to instruct and help everyone.

There was and still is a division distinguishing women by the portrayal of moral character. The kingdom women were marked by their modesty. They were trained to walk in purity. Heathen women were marked by immoral conduct and pagan worship. But, Jesus came to bridge the gap and bring both worlds together into holy living. We must dare to believe that Jesus is Lord over all and that His compassion will extend to even creatures of contemptible character when they repent and come to Him. You are called to excel.

Well, I pray you are convinced that there is a predestined virtuous image within you that is just longing to come out. I pray that you will listen to your heart's cry for a more abundant life and know that the more abundant life confidence comes from a relationship with God in obedience to His Word. God's Word and submission to the principles within it, will help you to explore all of the virtuous qualities within yourself and coach you through life to its rewards and victories. Now let me encourage you towards your unique virtuous image with a few pearls of wisdom. Remember,

1. God's compassion will bestow His mercy upon you everyday. He will be faithful to help you accomplish His will for your life.

2. God will cleanse you, give you his Spirit, and cause you to walk in his ways. Do not be discouraged.

3. God has equipped you with at least one gift to exercise in both the natural and supernatural realms of your life. Learn to use them well.

4. God will teach you how to govern your finances and increase them so that all your needs are met and His kingdom supported.

5. Assemble yourself with people who are sincere about their Christian life and will challenge your spiritual growth. Refrain from arguing issues concerning the Word, but search the scripture for truth concerning all matters.

6. Study the Word of God. Use other Christian literature to aid you in your spiritual insight, knowledge and growth. This will prevent you from falling into the hands of cults and the misguiding hands of disobedient leaders.

7. Do not compare your Christian growth and experiences to others as a measure of how much you are pleasing God. God's pleasure with you will come from you believing in His son Jesus and exercising your belief through obedience to His Word.

8. Be prepared to be separated from old friends for a season. This time will allow you to become a mature and capable witness of God's saving power. God will cause others to see how the power of God has changed your life. In return, He will open opportunities for you to share your faith with others. Additionally, patience will walk you into your primary gifts to support God's kingdom in the ministry you serve. Studying the Apostle Paul in Acts is a great witness to this truth and a source of encouragement.

9. Be confident in your new life with God. Jesus is praying for you right now. When old ways appear to be too hard to get rid of, don't despair. Go to God for help. He started the process of cleaning you up and He will continue until He comes to take us with Him.

10. Remember the consequence of sin is death. Don't surrender to the flirtation of sin's pleasure. It will at some point cause you

devastation. The one little fruit that was so pleasing and desirable to Eve, caused the whole world to reap sin and the penalty of death. Take drastic steps to expose and get rid of sin in your life. Then let God's Word reveal the way of truth and life.

11. God is not your enemy when things are not going the way you believe they should. God desires only good for your life. He will allow correction to come through trying difficulties. Yet, He is never out of control of your life. Keep the lines of communication open with Him through prayer.

12. Set spiritual and personal goals to be accomplished through a step-by-step progressive plan. It is good to broaden your education and work skills. Seek after that which would make you happy and will not compromise God's principles. For instance, if you wish to own a store, try owning a small or large grocery store, a clothing retail, or a kind of store that will be helpful to people. Do not desire anything (like a liquor store) that does not glorify God. By faith, you can and will accomplish your goals.

13. Love others around you as yourself. People come to Jesus because they need a Savior. Growing up in a Christian lifestyle is like starting your first day of school and having twelve grades of students ahead of you. Each grade has a level higher than its own even the twelfth grade. All students are still learning. Be as patient with others as you need them to be with you.

14. Pray! Pray! Pray! When one takes the time to sit and have a talk with God, it is better than talking to the greatest mother on earth. You invite Him to consume your being into fellowship with Him for the time you spend in prayer. In prayer, His voice gets clearer for you to recognize. His presence dispels fear, doubt, and

anxieties about failure. There, you will learn to worship Him and build confidence in your relationship with Him.

15. Obey God! Everyone knows that fire burns. Just get close enough to a burning flame and you will feel its heat. That heat will caution you to stay a certain distance from it or you will be burned. Not everyone has to receive a first, second, or third degree burn to know not to get to close to the fire. Sin is the same way. We don't have to always learn the consequences of sin through personal experiences. Stop following friends on general principles. Obey God!

Reference Scriptures to Study:

Lamentations 2:22-23

Isaiah 42:4-7

Isaiah 1:17

Acts 18:24-26

Timothy 2:15

Luke 23:42-43

Romans 8:1; 35-39

Jude 3:24

Romans 6:23

Jeremiah 29:11-14

Galatians 6:1-9

II Chronicles 7:14

Revelations 3:20

Ezekiel 36:25-30

Ephesians 4:8

Isaiah 48:17

Romans 14:1ll

John 21:21

Acts 9:1-18

Philippians 1:6

Genesis 3

John 14:6

Habakkuk 2:2-4

Luke 18:1

Acts 5:29-32

A Personal Prayer for You by Jesus

Jesus said these things. Then, raising his eyes in prayer, he said:

"Father, it's time. Display the bright splendor of your Son so the Son in turn may show your bright splendor. You put Him in charge of everything human so He might give real and eternal life to all in His charge.

And this is the real and eternal life: That they know you, The one and only true God, And Jesus Christ, whom you sent. I glorified you on earth by completing down to the last detail what you assigned me to do. And now, Father, glorify me with your very own splendor, the very splendor I had in your presence before there was a world.

I spelled out your character in detail to the men and women you gave me.

They were yours in the first place; Then you gave them to me, And they have now done what you said. They know now, beyond the shadow of a doubt, That everything you gave me is firsthand from you, For the message you gave me, I gave them; And they took it, and were convinced That I came from you. They believed that you sent me.

I pray for them. I'm not praying for the God-rejecting world, but for those you gave me,

For they are yours by right. Everything mine is yours, and yours mine, And my life is on display in them.

For I'm no longer going to be visible in the world; they'll continue in the world while I return to you.

Holy Father, guard them as they pursue this life that you conferred as a gift through me, So they can be one heart and mind as we are one heart and mind. As long as I was with them, I guarded them in the pursuit of the life you gave through me; I even posted a night watch. And not one of them got away, Except for the rebel bent on destruction.

Now I'm returning to you. I'm saying these things in the world's hearing so my people can experience my joy completed in them. I gave them your word;

The godless world hated them because of it, because they didn't join the world's ways, Just as I didn't join the world's ways. I'm not asking that you take them out of the world, but that you guard them from the Evil One.

They are no more defined by the world than I am defined by the world. Make them holy-consecrated-with the truth; Your word is consecrating truth.

In the same way that you gave me a mission in the world, I give them a mission in the world. I'm consecrating myself for their sakes so they'll be truth consecrated in their mission.

I'm praying not only for them, but also for those who will believe in me because of them and their witness about me. The goal is for all of them to become one heart and mind.

Just as you, Father, are in me and I in you, so they might be one heart and mind with us. Then the world might believe that you, in fact, sent me.

The same glory you gave me, I gave them, so they'll be as unified and together as we are- I in them and you in me. Then they'll be mature in this oneness, and give the godless world evidence that you've sent me and loved them in the same way you've loved me.

Father, I want those you gave me to be with me, right where I am, so they can see my glory, the splendor you gave me, having loved me long before there ever was a world. Righteous Father, the world has never known you, but I have known you, and these disciples know that you sent me on this mission. I have made your very being known to them-Who you are and what you do and continue to make it know, so that your love for me might be in them-exactly as I am in them." John 17 - The Message by Eugene H. Peterson

Be It unto You According to Your Faith

About the Author

Pastor Cynthia E. J. Carter

One of her most favored scriptures in the Bible is:

"He shall not fail nor be discouraged, till he have

set judgment in the earth and the isles shall wait

for his law" (Isaiah 42:4).

At the age of thirteen, she was an 8th grade dropout, a runaway and was among pimps, prostitutes, and drug dealers (your imagination can paint the picture of her life). God delivered her from this atmosphere through her mother and Juvenile Detention intervention, and she was saved at the age of seventeen. Being saved was a joy, but overcoming the struggles of her past, living holy, and living up to all of her God given potential was a struggle. Among other scriptures in the Bible, Isaiah 42:4 changed her life.

She felt if God's Spirit could uphold Jesus through all the trials and pains of the cross, surely he could complete his work in her.

Accomplishments

Pastor Carter has been preaching the Gospel of Jesus Christ since 1991. She has served as a chaplain in the Harris County Juvenile Detention Center under the umbrella of Youth for Christ and has preached in Women's Correctional Institutions in the states of Texas, Florida and Virginia.

Pastor Carter is the founder and Sr. Pastor of Word Under the Stars Ministries, Inc. better known as, "WUTS". This ministry is serving communities through the heart of evangelism since 2001 and is located in Houston, Texas. She is a Board Certified Belief Therapist through the Therapon Institute and a Certified Christian Marriage & Family Therapist. She is a Certified Christian Counselor and Life Coach. She holds an Honorary Doctor of Divinity Degree by CICA International University & Seminary and a Degree of Leadership Studies through Elect Lady Sons of Thunder School of Ministry & Mentoring Academy. Pastor Carter believes, "The neighborhood should be able to see and experience the life changing effects of the ministry of Jesus Christ through the local Church".

She has written many books that are in the process of being published. Her plan is to use the books in her ministry of preaching and teaching to hurting people across the world. Her goal is to encourage men and women letting them know there is hope in Christ Jesus. Her desire is to evangelize the neighborhoods and reach as many unsaved people as possible through this book. She prays for as many believers as led by God to share in this Kingdom building effort.

A Special Thank you to Sponsors Who Financially Supported the Publishing of This Book. May God Bless You for Believing and Supporting This Project!!!

Dr. Marsha Y. Jordan

Mother Mary Parker

Pastor Sandra Mosley

Evangelist Sylvia Page

Sis. Norma Williams

Min. Doris Thomas

Sis. Winnie Green

Sis. Janet Craft

Evangelist Marvin Powell

Evangelist Barbara J. Still

Sis. Jacqueline Britton

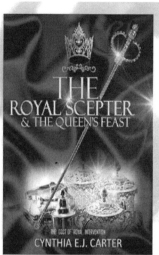

Honey Out of A Dead Carcass $14.95
Honey Out of A Dead Carcass WKBK $12.95
SET - Book and Workbook $25.00

Pray it 100 Times: Fear Not!
$9.95

Portraits Of A Woman
Workshop Kit

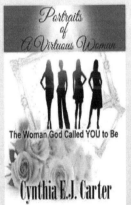

PVW Workshop Complete: $299.95
1 Facilitator's PWV Workshop Guide Complete
19 Activity Posters (2 per workshop and 1 for 10th
workshop)
2 Group Activity Puzzles
5 PVW Books
5 PVW Workbook Study Guides
(This does not include Answer posters until I can really price
them - the posters wholesale will cost approximately
$7 ea: this is roughly $207.50 to print not including
ship/package)

Made in the USA
Columbia, SC
30 November 2023

27475976R00098